Contents

Teacher's Introduction

	Worksheet	Activity	Level	Time	Aim	Language
19	Opposites 2	Whole class/ Pairwork	High beginners	20	To teach adjectives	everyday nouns and adjectives
20	Tic Tac Toe 2	Groupwork	High beginners	30	To ask tag questions	*..., isn't he? ..., haven't you? ..., aren't they? ..., will you? ...,* etc.
21	The Alien	Whole class	Low beginners	30	To ask questions	*Is he/she/it ... ? Does he/she/it ... ? What ... ? How old ... ?*
22	When was the last time you ...?	Pairwork	High beginners	25	To use the past tense with expressions of time	*last night/day/week/month/year x days/weeks/months/years ago the day before*
23	"A kind of" Crossword Puzzle	Pairwork	High beginners	30	To practice spelling	words beginning with 'c'
24	It's Debatable	Pairwork	Intermediate	60	To practice fluency	statements of opinion and disagreeing
25	What's the Question?	Whole class	High beginners	20	To form *Wh-* questions	*Who, What, When, Where, What kind of, How many?* etc.
26	Caption it!	Whole class	High beginners	30	To write descriptive phrases	nouns to identify people *- ing* form for activities
27	Intern Psychologist	Whole class	High beginners	45	To practice describing things	adjectives of size, condition, feeling, etc
28	When was the first time you ...?	Pairwork	Low intermediate	25	To refer to the past	simple past time expressions
29	Education	Whole class/ Pairwork	Low intermediate	25	To recognise word families	nouns ending in *-ation, -tion,* or *-ion*
30	Irregular Verb Word Search 2	Whole class/ Pairwork	High beginners	30	To practice irregular verbs	irregular verbs
31	Postcards	Pairwork	High beginners	30	To compose simple messages	positive and negative adjectives vacations
32	Dial-a-Word	Pairwork/ Groupwork	Beginners	30	To spell and say numbers	letters and numbers
33	Class Models	Pairwork	High beginners	25	To give instructions	verbs of movement parts of the body instructions
34	Mini-summit	Whole class/ Pairwork	Beginners	20	To review standard greetings/farewells	greetings, introductions, farewells
35	Synchronized English	Pairwork	High beginners	45	To give and respond to instructions	parts of the body instructions
36	I Bet You Can't	Pairwork	Beginners	30	To review parts of the body	parts of the body

Contributors/Questionnaire

Ready-made English

Ready-made English

1

Multi-level activities

edited
Kurt Scheibner

Heinemann

Heinemann English Language Teaching

A division of Reed Educational and Professional Publishing Limited
Halley Court, Jordan Hill, Oxford OX2 8EJ

OXFORD MADRID FLORENCE ATHENS PRAGUE SÃO PAULO MEXICO CITY
CHICAGO PORTSMOUTH (NH) SINGAPORE KUALA LUMPUR
MELBOURNE AUCKLAND JOHANNESBURG IBADAN GABORONE

ISBN 0 435 24168 0

Text © North Star Publishing Company 1995
Design and illustration © Heinemann Publishers (Oxford) Ltd. 1995
First published in Japan as *Prism*
This edition first published 1995

Designed by Kevin McGeoghegan and Alix Harrower
Cover design by Stafford & Stafford
Illustrated by: Philip Bannister, Roger Fereday and Celia Canning

Printed in Great Britain by Thomson Litho, East Kilbride, Scotland
Bound by Hunter and Foulis, Edinburgh, Scotland

96 97 98 99 10 9 8 7 6 5 4 3 2

Teacher's Introduction

Ready-made English contains worksheets and accompanying Teacher's Notes for 36 speaking activities for ESL/EFL students. The lessons, which can be done in any order, have been extensively piloted and developed in the classroom to ensure maximum motivation and enjoyment on the part of the student and consistent ease of use for the teacher.

Ready-made English can be used to supplement coursework on individual language items and skills, to provide communicative extension material for all-round language improvement and to encourage a class in its awareness of language as a social tool. All classes will benefit from a variety of enjoyable activities being added to a course and **Ready-made English** is flexible enough to complement all main coursebooks.

Using **Ready-made English** in the classroom

The Teacher's Notes for each activity are easy to follow so that an appropriate activity for any classroom situation can be selected.

Displayed along the left margin are these items:

Activity   refers to classroom organization into pairs, groups or as a whole class.

Level   indicates the level of English ability a student should have (Beginner to Intermediate) in order to participate fully in the activity. Each lesson, however, is easily adjustable for higher or lower level students.

Time   gives an approximate amount of time required to do the activity.

The body of the Teacher's Notes pages contains these items:

Aim   describes the teaching objective.

Language   outlines a list of the targeted structures and/or vocabulary.

Preparation   includes suggestions on preparation and pre-teaching as well as helpful suggestions on how to lead the students smoothly into the worksheet pages.

Procedure   offers a step-by-step explanation of how to do the lesson.

Variations   suggests different ways of extending the material for higher or lower level students by introducing additional language skills.

Further Practice   presents ways of expanding the activity for greater writing and/or discussion reinforcement and often cross-refers to other worksheets with a similar aim or topic.

Acknowledgements

This collection of lessons includes many of the editor's favorites and some original and creative lessons contributed by other teachers of ESL/EFL.

Sincere appreciation is expressed to Kelley Seymour and Robert Jenkins, without whose creativity and hard work this book may never have come into being. Also the editor would like to thank Vaughan Jones of Heinemann, who discovered the material in its original form and faithfully supported it right up to publication in its present version. Finally, perhaps the greatest thanks must go to the hundreds of "guinea-pig" students who were the best critics.

World Population Cards

Aim

To practice the use of large numbers as approximate or precise figures.

Language

Yes/No questions using *Are there …?*

Numbers over one million

more than/less than/just

Preparation

Prior to class, copy and cut the cards from Worksheet 1. These cards give approximate populations of ten cities and ten countries. Begin by reviewing (or teaching) how to say large numbers in English. Write a single digit on the board, for example *8*. Have the students say the number. To the left of the *8* write another number, for example *3*. Have students say *thirty-eight*. Write another number to the left, for example *6* and have students say *six hundred and thirty-eight*. Add another number to the left. This time, draw a vertical line and write the word *thousand* to the left of the line and below the new number. Have the students read *two thousand, six hundred and thirty-eight*. Continue writing one more digit to the left drawing a vertical line to separate the millions and the billions. Each time, have the students say the number.

Procedure

1. Give one card to a student and have him/her come to the front of the room.

2. Divide the other students into teams and have each team, in turn, ask questions to determine the exact population of the city or country as written on the card. Teams should ask questions using the words *more than*, *less than*, or *just*. For example, *Are there more than 5 million people living in Paris?* The student with the card either says *Yes* or *No*.

3. If the answer is *Yes*, the same team continues asking questions. If the answer is *No*, the question is passed to the next team.

4. Teams continue asking questions until the population – as printed on the card – has been arrived at. Award a point to the team that correctly asks: *Are there just 8,687,227 people living in Paris?*

Variations

1. Have one student stand at the board and a second student say the name of his/her hometown, parent's or grandparent's hometown. The student at the board writes down the name. The second student estimates the population of his/her home town, writes it down and the other students guess.

2. Make two copies of Worksheet 1 and on one blank out the first, third, fifth, etc. population figures and on the other the second, fourth, sixth, etc. population figures. Title one page A and the other B. Make enough copies for every student. In class, pair the students, hand out copies of A and B respectively and have them ask each other for the missing information.

Further Practice

Hand each student a card and have him or her assume the role of someone living in that city or country. As part of the roleplay have students agree to be pen pals with other students in class and actually have them write a few letters back and forth. Encourage students to research their cities or countries so they can relay realistic news about the culture, conditions, schools, jobs, families, etc.

World Population Cards ①

Moscow 9,540,063 **City**	**Tokyo** 19,279,488 **City**	**India** 853,372,000 Country	**United States** 249,235,000 Country
Mexico City 20,258,230 **City**	**Shanghai** 12,351,940 **City**	**France** 56,173,000 Country	**United Kingdom** 56,926,000 Country
London 10,406,040 **City**	**Rome** 3,756,414 **City**	**China** 1,135,495,000 Country	**Mexico** 88,597,000 Country
Calcutta 12,545,650 **City**	**Paris** 8,687,227 **City**	**Canada** 26,525,000 Country	**Japan** 127,456,000 Country
Bangkok 7,380,509 **City**	**New York** 15,691,039 **City**	**Australia** 16,745,000 Country	**Italy** 57,321,000 Country

PHOTOCOPIABLE

World Populations

Aim

To work with large numbers, asking and answering questions about populations.

Language

What … do you have?

How many people live in …?

There are …

Numbers over one million

Preparation

It is important to teach the concept of large numbers before launching into this activity. Review thousands, millions and billions before beginning this lesson. (See Worksheet 1.) Review the questions and answers written at the top of Worksheet 2. Also, review the questions written at the bottom: *How do you spell …?* and *Would you repeat that, please?*

Prior to class, copy and cut the cards from Worksheet 1. With classes of more than 20 students, make more than one set of cards.

Procedure

1. Hand out one copy of Worksheet 2 to each student.

2. Hand out one, two or three World Population cards to each student (depending on the size of the class) and explain that this activity is a race. The object is to write down all of the names of the cities and countries and their corresponding populations.

3. First, ask students to write down on the worksheet the information about their own city or country (i.e., the card(s) they are holding).

Variations

1. This could be done as a pairwork by giving each student in the pair half of the cards. Together they exchange all of the information in order to complete their worksheet.

2. Have groups of students work in pairs but seated apart from each other so that they have to raise their voices to be heard by their partners. This is a great way to build a lot of energy in the classroom.

3. This lesson can easily be changed to practice past or future tenses as well. Find an atlas of populations cited 50 or 100 years ago or with predictions of populations in the future. Make new cards with these numbers so that students can practice past or future tenses.

World Populations

Q: What city or country do you have?

A: I have _____.

Q: How many people live in _____?

A: There are _____ people living in _____.

City	Population	Country	Population
1. _____ _____	1. _____ _____
2. _____ _____	2. _____ _____
3. _____ _____	3. _____ _____
4. _____ _____	4. _____ _____
5. _____ _____	5. _____ _____
6. _____ _____	6. _____ _____
7. _____ _____	7. _____ _____
8. _____ _____	8. _____ _____
9. _____ _____	9. _____ _____
10. _____ _____	10. _____ _____

How do you spell _____?   Would you repeat that, please?

©North Star Publishing Co. 1995
Published by Heinemann English Language Teaching. This sheet may be photocopied and used within the class.

Sentence Links

Aim

To build the confidence of lower ability students by enabling them to make a long, complete and correct sentence in English.

Language

Past tense of *go*

Prepositions: *to* (direction), *by*, *at* (with time), *on* (with days), *to* (for purpose), *with*

Vocabulary of places, means of transport, activities

Preparation

This exercise builds the confidence of lower-level English speakers. In just a few minutes, students will be able to construct a correct English sentence by stringing together a sentence of six phrases by drawing on vocabulary they already know. If students know the words *went to*, *by*, *at*, *on*, *to* and *with*, they can do this lesson quite comfortably.

Draw a diagram on the board similar to that shown on Worksheet 3.

Procedure

1. Explain the meaning of each of the *sentence parts* (Student's name, Place, Transportation, etc.). Have students offer appropriate words to fill in the boxes.

2. Read the first two *sentence parts* as provided by the students. For example: *Harvey, Toronto*. Explain that *Harvey Toronto* is not a sentence. There is no verb, but if these two words are linked with *went to*, then *Harvey went to Toronto* becomes a complete sentence.

3. Continue to the third sentence part. For example, *Harvey went to Toronto canoe*, is an incomplete sentence. Ask students to supply the missing link *by* to make the sentence complete, i.e. *Harvey went to Toronto by canoe*.

4. Continue item by item with the students supplying the missing words. Students will see the development of the sentence as it grows.

5. When finished, have the whole class read out the complete sentence. (Notice that only Pattern 1 has been used up to this point. Patterns 2 and 3 will come later.)

6. At this point, break the class into pairs and hand out Worksheet 3. Go through the model sentence at the top. Then refer to Patterns 1, 2 and 3. Point out that each box has a letter, from A to U. Have one student turn over his/her paper. The other, starting with A, asks *Give me a student's name*. The response is written in the appropriate box. Then continue on to B, C and D until all are filled in.

7. When both partners have written appropriate responses in each of the boxes, have one student read his/her Pattern 1 sentence, including the links. Then the other student reads Pattern 1. Students alternate reading through all three patterns.

Variations

1. Have the students create a completely new sentence by rotating their answers, e.g. one student reads from the first box, another student reads from the second box, etc.

2. Turn this lesson into a pairwork, question/response activity. When all of the boxes have been filled in, hand out another sheet to all students. Student A asks *Who...?* and Student B reads the student's name from the first box. Student A records the name on the new sheet. Then Student A asks in order *Where did he/she go? How did he/she go? How did he/she get there? At what time? On what day? To do what?* and finally *With whom?*

3. Hand out one *Who am I* card (Worksheets 6a and 6b) to each student to use for the Famous person sentence part.

SENTENCE LINKS

Model Sentence

Student's name		Place		Transportation		Time of day		Date/Day		Activity		Famous person
Harvey	went to	*Toronto*	by	*canoe*	at	*3:56 p.m.*	on	*May 17th*	to	*water-ski*	with	*Cleopatra.*
	Link		Link		Link		Link		Link		Link	

Harvey went to Toronto by canoe at 3:56 p.m. on May 17th to water-ski with Cleopatra.

Pattern 1

Student's name	Place	Transportation	Time of day	Date/Day	Activity	Famous person
A	B	K	R	M	D	T

Pattern 2

Student's name	Famous person	Place	Transportation	Activity	Time of day	Date/Day
P	F	C	I	O	G	H

Pattern 3

Date/Day	Famous person	Place	Transportation	Time of day	Activity	Student's name
J	U	E	Q	L	S	N

Irregular Verb Word Search 1

Aim

To practice present and past tense forms of irregular verbs.

Language

Some common irregular verbs

Preparation

Students approaching this exercise should be well grounded in the basic 80 or 90 English verbs and know their present and past tense forms. This word search puzzle is useful as a reinforcement of their knowledge. Before handing out Worksheet 4, read down the list of verbs in the present tense and have students say their past tense form. (This could be done in teams to make this part competitive, giving a point to the team which answers first.)

Also, teach the following three words: *horizontal(ly)*, *vertical(ly)* and *diagonal(ly)*.

Procedure

1. Pair the students and have them fold their papers along the dotted line separating part A from part B.

2. One student looks at the word search puzzle at the top, the other looks at the verbs at the bottom. Student B begins by asking: *What's the past tense of beat?* Student A responds with: *(The past tense of beat is) beat.*

3. Then Student A looks for the word *beat* which is printed somewhere in the puzzle. If Student A has trouble finding the word, he/she can ask for a hint: *Where is it?* Student B looks at the hint as printed on his/her paper: A1–h and responds with: *It begins on A1 and goes horizontally.*

Variations

1. As a whole class (or competitive group) activity, appoint one student to be the MC and hand one copy to each of the other students. Have everyone fold the papers horizontally and all but the MC look at Part A. The MC looks only at Part B. The MC reads the present tense verbs and students search for their past tense forms. When each is found, the student reveals its location by saying, for example: *It begins on H13 and goes diagonally.* The MC confirms the answer.

2. This can be done as a take-home assignment but before making copies, blank out the hints from part B (otherwise it's too easy).

Answers

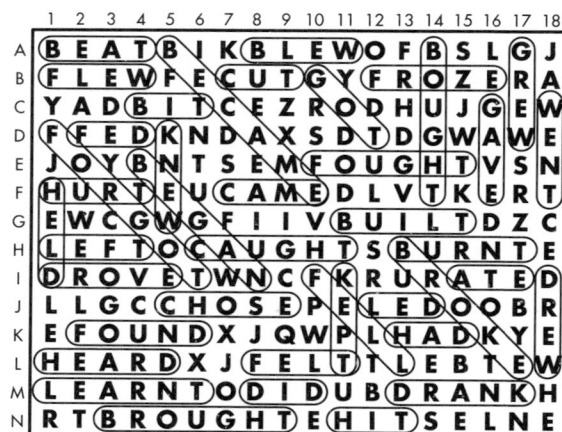

Further Practice

See *Irregular Verb Word Search 2*, Worksheet 30.

Irregular Verb Word Search 1

(4)

A

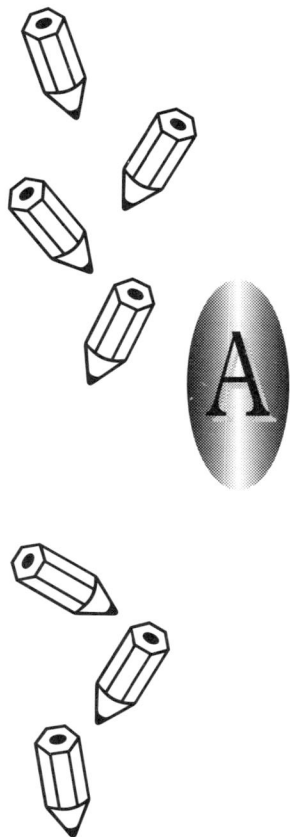

	1	2	3	4	5	6	7	8	9	10	11	12	13	14	15	16	17	18
A	B	E	A	T	B	I	K	B	L	E	W	O	F	B	S	L	G	J
B	F	L	E	W	F	E	C	U	T	G	Y	F	R	O	Z	E	R	A
C	Y	A	D	B	I	T	C	E	Z	R	O	D	H	U	J	G	E	W
D	F	F	E	D	K	N	D	A	X	S	D	T	D	G	W	A	W	E
E	J	O	Y	B	N	T	S	E	M	F	O	U	G	H	T	V	S	N
F	H	U	R	T	E	U	C	A	M	E	D	L	V	T	K	E	R	T
G	E	W	C	G	W	G	F	I	I	V	B	U	I	L	T	D	Z	C
H	L	E	F	T	O	C	A	U	G	H	T	S	B	U	R	N	T	E
I	D	R	O	V	E	T	W	N	C	F	K	R	U	R	A	T	E	D
J	L	L	G	C	C	H	O	S	E	P	E	L	E	D	O	O	B	R
K	E	F	O	U	N	D	X	J	Q	W	P	L	H	A	D	K	Y	E
L	H	E	A	R	D	X	J	F	E	L	T	T	L	E	B	T	E	W
M	L	E	A	R	N	T	O	D	I	D	U	B	D	R	A	N	K	H
N	R	T	B	R	O	U	G	H	T	E	H	I	T	S	E	L	N	E

horizontal ←---→   vertical ↕   diagonal ↖↘

B — Hints & Answers

	Present Tense	Past Tense		Present Tense	Past Tense		Present Tense	Past Tense
A1–h	beat	*beat*	M8–h	do		C16–v	give	
A5–d	become	*became*	I18–v	draw		C18–v	go	
E4–d	begin		M13–h	drink		A17–v	grow	
C4–h	bite		I1–h	drive		K13–h	have	
A8–h	blow		I15–h	eat		L1–h	hear	
N3–h	bring		I10–d	fall		N11–h	hit	
H13–d	break		D2–h	feed		F1–v	hold	
G11–h	build		L8–h	feel		F1–h	hurt	
H13–h	burn		E10–h	fight		I11–v	keep	
A14–v	buy		K2–h	find		D5–v	know	
H6–h	catch		B1–h	fly		J12–h	lead	
J5–h	choose		B12–h	freeze		M1–h	learn	
F7–h	come		D1–d	forget		H1–h	leave	
B7–h	cut		B10–d	get				

h=horizontal ←---→   v=vertical ↕   d=diagonal ↖↘

©North Star Publishing Co. 1995
Published by Heinemann English Language Teaching. This sheet may be photocopied and used within the class.

PHOTOCOPIABLE

Likes and Dislikes

Aim

To enquire about personal likes and dislikes and to reply by expressing varying degrees of feeling.

Language

Do you/Does he/she like ...?

I love/like/hate ... -ing + ways of expressing intermediate stages

Preparation

Begin by reviewing the eight responses listed at the top of Worksheets 5a and 5b. Ask a few *Do you like...?* questions to the class and have students answer in complete sentences. For example: *Do you like fishing?* Students should answer with one of the eight responses, for example: *Yes, I love fishing, Yes, I kind of like fishing, No, I don't like fishing very much,* etc. Explain the differences in subtlety between the meaning of each of the eight responses.

Procedure

1. Pair the students and hand out one copy (either Worksheet 5a or 5b respectively) to each student. (If the students are sitting in a circle, hand out the papers in the order of A, B, B, A, A, B).

2. Students write one *Do you like ...?* question of their own on line 14.

3. Without looking at each other's papers, the students should begin asking the questions and marking the answers by writing an X or some other mark in the appropriate column.

4. When all of the pairs have finished, have them switch partners so that all of the new pairs will have the same copy, i.e. A+A or B+B. Have students ask their new partners (using a new mark): *Does he/she like walking in the rain?* (This is good practice using the third person pronoun.)

Variations

1. If time, have the A+A and B+B pairs practice Part 1 together, i.e. *Do you like ...?* and use a third mark to indicate the new response.

2. Introduce how to change from the gerund to the infinitive form. Help students practice saying *Do you like to walk in the rain?*

3. Use this lesson to review phrases such as *me too, so do I, I don't either, neither do I,* etc.

Further Practice

Have students write short sentences using the word *because*. For example, *I really like staying up late because ...* or *I don't like cleaning my room because ... .*

Likes & Dislikes

Do you like …	Yes, I love …	Yes, I really like …	Yes, I like …	Yes, I kind of like …	No, I don't really like …	No, I don't like … very much.	No, I don't like …	No, I hate …
1. walking in the rain?							✗	
2. swimming?								
3. cooking?								
4. staying up late at night?								
5. shopping?								
6. listening to jazz?								
7. going to the zoo?								
8. studying English?								
9. writing letters?								
10. going to parties?								
11. camping?								
12. visiting relatives?								
13. sleeping?								
14. _____?								

©North Star Publishing Co. 1995
Published by Heinemann English Language Teaching. This sheet may be photocopied and used within the class.

Likes & Dislikes

Do you like ...

	Yes, I love ...	Yes, I really like ...	Yes, I like ...	Yes, I kind of like ...	No, I don't really like ...	No, I don't like ... very much.	No, I don't like ...	No, I hate ...
1. cleaning your room?					✗			
2. reading the newspaper?								
3. talking on the telephone?								
4. waking up early?								
5. jogging?								
6. watching movies?								
7. doing homework?								
8. listening to opera?								
9. playing tennis?								
10. singing in the shower?								
11. flying in an airplane?								
12. washing dishes?								
13. fishing?								
14. _____?								

©North Star Publishing Co. 1995
Published by Heinemann English Language Teaching. This sheet may be photocopied and used within the class.

Who am I?

Mickey Mouse

Einstein[2]

Tarzan

Cleopatra

Frank Sinatra

Frankenstein

Snow White

Harrison Ford

Minnie Mouse

Peter Pan

Who am I?

Aim

To encourage communication between all students asking open and closed questions.

Language

Simple open and closed questions in past and present tenses

Preparation

There are several ways to do this simple, fun activity for all levels of students. Copy Worksheets 6a and 6b and cut the pages into separate cards.

In class, begin with a demonstration of this activity by having students think of a famous person. The teacher tries to find out who it is by asking various model questions.

Procedure

1. Tape or pin one card to the back of each student.

2. Without students knowing their new identities, have them go around asking questions such as *When was I famous? Why was I famous? What are my initials?* etc.

3. Encourage students to ask only one question per classmate then continue circulating.

Variations

1. Have students ask questions that require a *Yes* or *No* response such as *Am/Was I a woman? Am I living? Did I write books? Am/Was I a famous sports personality?*

2. Repeat the activity when finished, but this time have students write a famous person's name on the back of the card and attach it to a classmate.

3. *Who Are You?* Students know their identities (cards are hidden), but the others don't. Students ask *Yes* or *No* questions to find out who the other students in the class are.

4. After identities have been discovered, put students into pairs and have them interview each other. For example, *Where do/did you live? Are/Were you European? Are/Were you a writer?*

5. After students find out who they are, have them ask questions to other students in class to find out something new about "themselves" that they didn't know before. Report this finding to the class.

Note: One blank card is included for the teacher to write in a name of someone famous – or even write in the name of one of the students.

Further Practice

1. Encourage students to compose a mini-research project about their famous person. These could be read aloud in class or simply given to the teacher as a writing project.

2. Use these cards, interview style, to fill out the *Personal Information Sheet* (Worksheet 12).

Who am I?

Beethoven

Helen Keller

Charlie Chaplin

Dracula

Thomas Edison

Zeus

Mother Theresa

King Kong

 SHAKESPEARE

Opposites 1

Aim

To expand the vocabulary of lower ability students by practicing adjectives listed as pairs of opposites.

Language

60 simple adjectives

Preparation

This list of opposites includes common adjectives. It is especially intended for beginning students and is a great pairwork or whole class confidence builder. To establish a stronger vocabulary base, students can usually attach *not* to most of these words, thus doubling their ability to have a conversation. For example, if a student does not know the opposite of *far*, there is always the safe description that something is *not far*. The subtlety between *near* and *not far* probably is not terrifically important among beginning students.

Procedure

1. Give each student in class a copy of Worksheet 7.

2. Start by going down the list to check for understanding by saying the word and asking for synonyms or examples of its meanings. Students will need to know the meaning of all the words before they can proceed with this lesson.

3. Next, divide the class into two or three groups. Read the first word off the list. Whichever group supplies an appropriate opposite gets a point. The group with the most points at the end is the winner. For higher level classes, students must put the opposite word in a sentence to get a point.

Variations

1. Use these words for *Password* (Worksheets 13a–d) once students have learned them.

2. For listening practice, do the lesson without handing out the paper first.

3. As a pairwork activity, have one student cover up the right list and the other the left.

4. Encourage students to make sentences using opposites, e.g. *My neighbor is rich but my cousin is poor.*

Further Practice

1. Pair students and have them compose sentences using two (or three) of the listed words in a single sentence. For example *The rich man took a long walk early in the morning.* Have pairs swap their sentences and write opposite sentences: *The poor man took a short walk late in the morning.*

2. As a writing exercise, have pairs of students compose a short story using either the left or right column of words.

3. Time the class to see how quickly they can go through the entire opposites list – without their papers. Make a note of the time and review the list occasionally, each time trying to reduce the time. With enough practice, students should be able to complete the list in under a minute.

Answers

rich – poor	male – female	married – single
long – short	first – last	round – square
early – late	high – low	front – back
good – bad	north – south	fast – slow
easy – difficult	cloudy – sunny/clear	smart – stupid/dull
best – worst	sick – healthy	off – on
wet – dry	left – right	cold – hot
black – white	old – new/young	clean – dirty
big – little/small	pretty – plain/ugly	fat – thin
sweet – sour/bitter	east – west	far – near

Opposites 1

fat	thin	sick	_____
long	_____	left	_____
early	_____	old	_____
good	_____	pretty	_____
easy	_____	east	_____
best	_____	married	_____
wet	_____	round	_____
black	_____	front	_____
big	_____	fast	_____
sweet	_____	smart	_____
male	_____	off	_____
first	_____	cold	_____
high	_____	clean	_____
north	_____	rich	_____
cloudy	_____	far	_____

©North Star Publishing Co. 1995
Published by Heinemann English Language Teaching. This sheet may be photocopied and used within the class.

Strip Quiz 1

Aim

To encourage students to tell a story by ordering sentences.

Language

Simple narrative in the past tense

Preparation

Prior to class, copy Worksheet 8 and cut into strips.

Markers are words that are used to signal sequential order and transition within a story. Students usually have little trouble organizing the parts of this story, but sometimes they need help in understanding which words controlled their choice.

Procedure

1. Divide the class into groups of seven and hand out the strips of paper. (If a small class, give some of the students two strips each.)

2. Without looking at each other's papers, the students should read their own strip(s) out at random and then discuss the order together until all the strips of paper are organized into the correct order.

3. When they have finished, explain that the story is actually a quiz. Encourage the students to ask questions such as *Is the size of the frogs important? Are the number of hops important?* If a student claims to have found the solution and says *I think the big frog is the adult*, ask him/her to explain.

Answer

See how long it takes to get the right answer, which is tricky. Both are adult frogs since a baby frog is a tadpole.

Variations

1. Have students stand in the correct order.

2. Have students memorize their strips.

Further Practice

See *Strip Quiz* 2 (Worksheet 15).

Strip Quiz 1

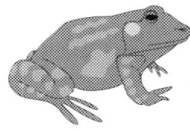

The Frogs

Two frogs were sitting in front of a large pond.

One was very big with brown and black skin.

The other frog was very small with all green skin.

The little frog said he could jump into the pond with only one hop.

Then the big frog said he could jump into the pond with only two hops.

They both jumped into the pond; the little frog needed one hop, the big frog needed two hops.

Which frog is an adult?

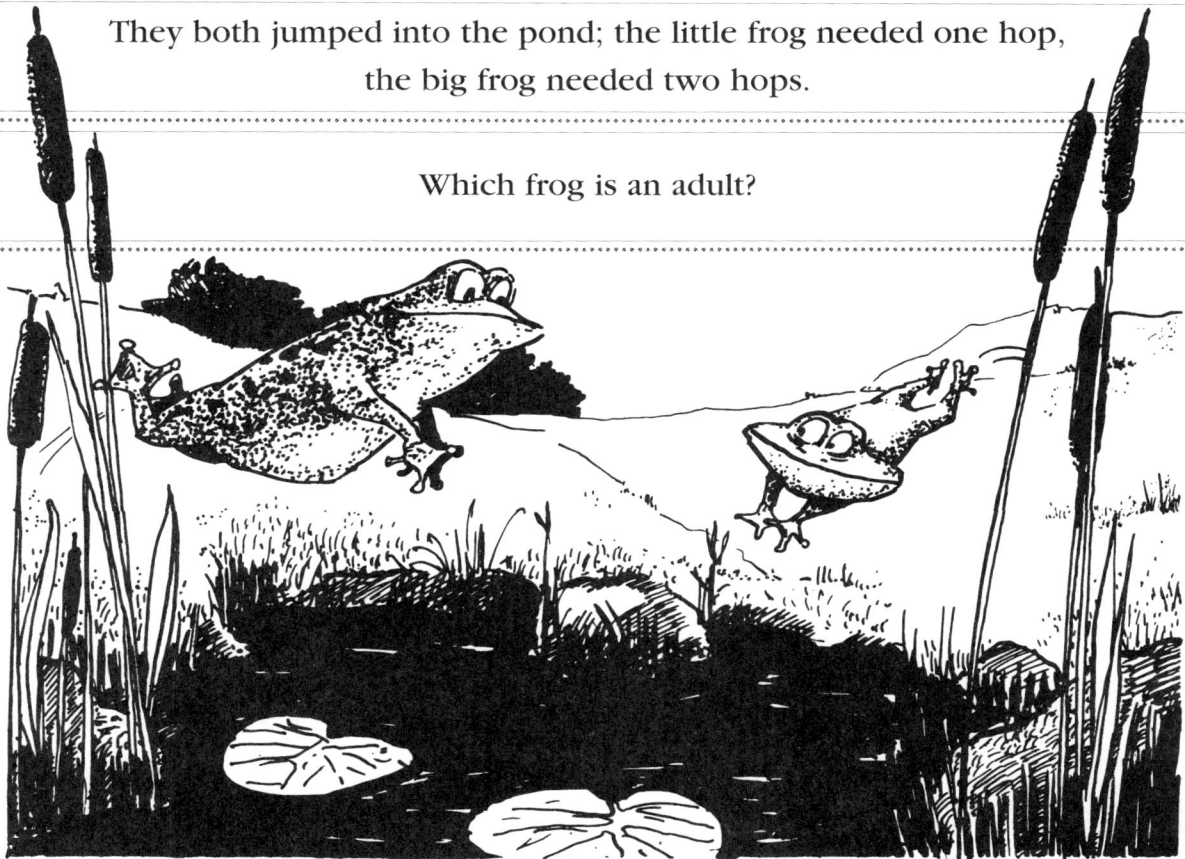

9

Find someone who...

Aim

To introduce members of a new class to each other and to practice asking closed questions in the simple present.

Language

Do you ...?

Yes, I do/No, I don't

Vocabulary of everyday activities

Preparation

This works well with a new class because students not only practice a simple English pattern, they also find out the names of their classmates. Since the only question being asked is *Do you ...?*, even beginning students can feel quite confident doing this activity. Explain the *Do you ...?* question and the appropriate answers, i.e. *Yes, I do* or *No, I don't*. Some students may try responding with *Sometimes*; this should be accepted as an affirmative answer.

Procedure

1. Copy and hand out Worksheet 9 and have students create their own *Do you ...?* question on line 15.

2. Then have students go around the class and try to find someone who can give a positive answer to one of the 15 questions.

3. When students find someone who answers *Yes, I do*, the respondent should sign his/her own full name on the sheet. [The object is to fill up the sheet as quickly, and with as many different signatures, as possible. This is an active lesson and the students will be running around the room asking everyone all of the *Do you ...?* questions.]

Variations

1. When they have finished, pair the students and have them ask each other questions like *Does Sharon play tennis once a month?* The responses can be *Yes, she does*, *No, she doesn't*, or *I don't know*.

2. The teacher asks, after everyone has finished, *Who plays tennis once a month?* Students answer by saying *Robert does*, or *Everyone does*, or *No one does*.

3. Encourage students to ask one follow-up question before moving on to another classmate. This will help them to circulate among themselves better.

Further Practice

1. For practice of *Do you ...?* type questions, see *Likes and Dislikes* (Worksheets 5a and 5b).

2. This lesson works well as an introduction to *When was the first time you ...?* (Worksheets 28a and 28b) and *When was the last time you ...?* (Worksheets 22a and 22b).

3. Pair students and have each pair compose a list of three additional *Do you ...?* questions. Then have all the students ask the rest of the class their new questions.

4. Have students title a piece of paper *The reasons why I ...*. Have them make a list of three reasons why they do one of the items on the list. When they have finished, pair the students and have them make this into a guessing-style conversation where partners try to arrive at the three reasons.

Find someone who ...

Questions	Answers
Do you ...?	Yes, I do. *or* No, I don't.

Do you ...?  *Name*

1. ... play tennis once a month? _____

2. ... like to wake up early? _____

3. ... study English every day? _____

4. ... collect stamps? _____

5. ... live alone? _____

6. ... like to cook?  _____

7. ... have a motorcycle? _____

8. ... wear contact lenses? _____

9. ... often clean your room?  _____

10. ... read a newspaper every day? _____

11. ... snore?  _____

12. ... like your name? _____

13. ... watch TV every day? _____

14. ... speak two languages? _____

15. ... _____? _____

©North Star Publishing Co. 1995
Published by Heinemann English Language Teaching. This sheet may be photocopied and used within the class.

Tic Tac Toe 1

Aim

To practice asking *Wh-* questions.

Language

Who, What, When, Where, Why, How + all tenses

Preparation

This lesson reinforces students' knowledge and use of *Who, What, When, Where, Why* and *How* questions in a fun and competitive way.

Play a few games of regular nine-square Tic Tac Toe. Number the squares so that the students can identify the square of their choice by stating the number. Once students are familiar with the game, expand the number of squares to a grid containing 20 squares (see the worksheet). Pair or group the students and set up a mark for each, e.g. square, circle, triangle, star, etc. Draw these marks somewhere on the board.

The object of the game is to place three of the same marks in a continuous line either horizontally, vertically or diagonally. Copy and hand out Worksheet 10 and explain the rules.

Procedure

1. The starting team must ask a question to another team in the class. To be able to have its mark placed in one of the squares, the team must use correct English or no mark will be given. A minimum five-word question is suggested.

2. If the asking team's question uses correct English, the designated defending team must answer. An answer that is given in the wrong tense or uses incorrect English results in the loss of a turn. (The defending team does not get a mark regardless of the answer; only the questioning team has a chance for a mark.)

3. Rotate among the teams so each team, in turn, asks a question to another.

4. It may be best to determine a time limit (about 30 or 45 seconds) for composing questions and answers to keep the lesson active.

Variations

After a dozen rounds or so, the grid becomes pretty full of marks which makes winning very difficult. Explain that one team can challenge the mark of another team by asking a question. The rules are as follows:

1. If the challenging team's question uses correct English and the defending team's answer is also correct English, there is no change. For example, Team Y wants its mark on Square 13 where Team X already has its mark. In this case, Team Y challenges Team X by asking a *What kind of ...* question, e.g., *What kind of teeth did George Washington have?* If Team X replies *He had wooden teeth*, the challenge fails and there are no changes.

2. If the challenging team's question uses correct English but the answer is grammatically or factually incorrect, the defending team will lose one of its marks as decided by the challenging team. For example, Team Y asks *What kind of teeth did George Washington have?* If Team X responds with *He <u>has</u> wooden teeth* or *He had <u>stainless steel</u> teeth*, the mark is removed. (Note: Team Y cannot put its mark in the square; the space has only been cleared.)

3. If the challenging team's question uses incorrect English, the defending team need not answer. For example, *What kind of tooth did George Washington have?* In this case, Team X need not respond.

Further Practice

1. Have students write four or five complete questions by assigning them the horizontal or vertical rows, respectively. Later, pair the students and have them exchange papers and discuss or write out the answers to the questions.

2. Pick any four or five question starters from the grid and write them on the board. Have all of the students complete the questions.

3. See *Tic Tac Toe 2* (Worksheet 20).

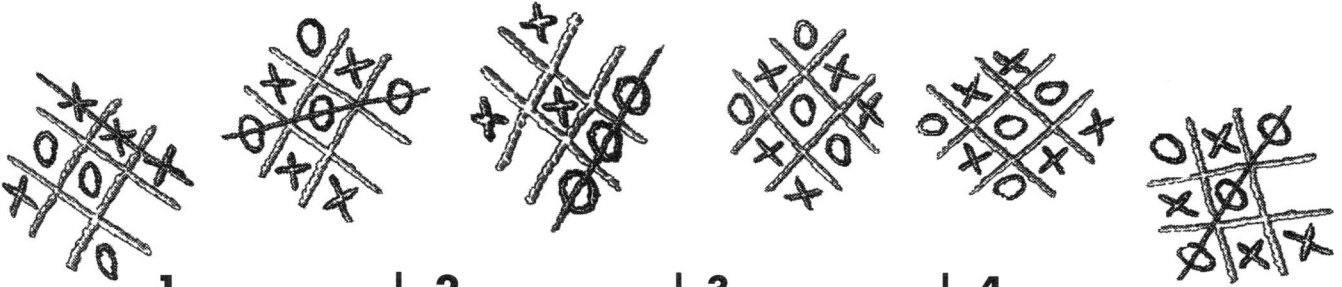

1. Who is …?	**2.** Why will …?	**3.** Where were …?	**4.** What was …?
5. When did …?	**6.** How many …?	**7.** Why were …?	**8.** Who was …?
9. Where is …?	**10.** What will …?	**11.** When was …?	**12.** How many …?
13. What kind of …?	**14.** Why is …?	**15.** Who will …?	**16.** Why did …?
17. How will …?	**18.** Who were …?	**19.** Where will …?	**20.** What did …?

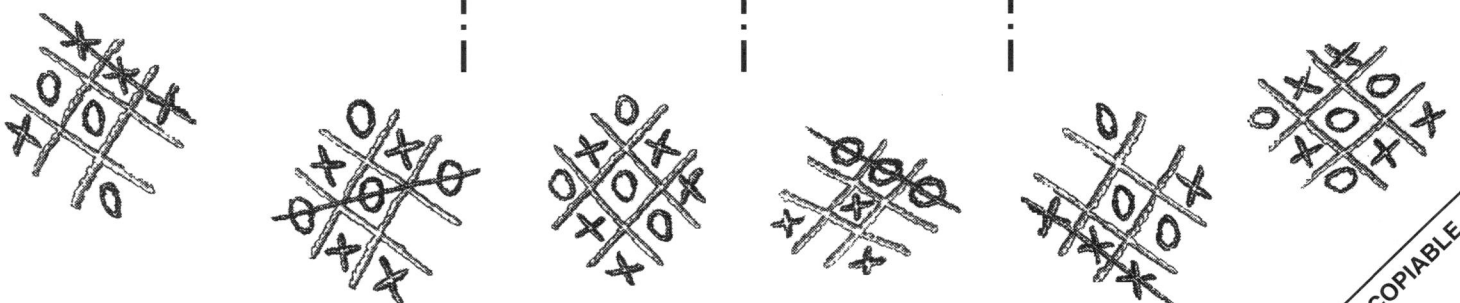

11 Sentence Tracks

Aim

To order words and sentences.

Language

Simple present narrative

Preparation

Copy Worksheet 11 onto an extra large piece of paper and cut each sentence into individual words (railroad cars). Keep these words together in a small envelope.

Make a note of any vocabulary that may be unknown to the students and before beginning this lesson, write these words on the board and go over their meanings.

Procedure

1. Divide the class into groups of four or five and give each group one of the sentences to put into order.

2. When the students have put the sentence into the correct order, have them write it down. Then give them a second sentence, then a third, etc., until they have put all of the sentences in their correct order.

3. Since the sentences themselves will be out of order, the final task will be to put the sentences into order. This is actually quite easy since all of the words within each sentence are numbered, but students do not always notice this.

4. Have the groups read the story in unison – a group or groups with a different sentence order will readily stand out.

Variations

1. If a large class, pin or tape one of the words from a sentence on each student and have them stand in the correct order with the other students after compiling the sentence.

2. With a large class, i.e., enough for eight groups, hand out the entire story, one set of sentences per group. Have groups race to put the entire story into order.

3. Prior to copying the worksheet, white out all the numbers. Copy and cut the words into sets as explained above. Keep the words in their original sets, but without numbers; students will have to put the sentences into order as well.

4. Selectively remove some of the words from each sentence, for example the verbs or the pronouns. Have students identify where a word is missing then suggest an appropriate replacement.

Further Practice

Have the whole class read the story in unison – but in the past, the past perfect or the past continuous tense.

Sentence Tracks

A¹ man¹ lives¹ in¹ the¹ desert¹ and¹ wants¹ some¹ water¹ for¹ his¹ bean¹ plants¹.

It² doesn't² rain² for² three² years² and² he² gets² very² hungry².

He³ prays³ to³ the³ gods³ for³ rain³ but³ nothing³ happens³.

He⁴ walks⁴ to⁴ a⁴ desert⁴ temple⁴ and⁴ talks⁴ to⁴ a⁴ wise⁴ old⁴ man⁴.

The⁵ old⁵ man⁵ says⁵, "Be⁵ patient⁵ and⁵ don't⁵ worry⁵."

On⁶ the⁶ way⁶ home⁶ he⁶ starts⁶ to⁶ cry⁶.

He⁷ cries⁷ so⁷ much⁷ that⁷ he⁷ makes⁷ a⁷ river⁷ of⁷ tears⁷.

Now⁸ he⁸ has⁸ enough⁸ water⁸ to⁸ feed⁸ his⁸ bean⁸ plants⁸.

PHOTOCOPIABLE

©North Star Publishing Co. 1995
Published by Heinemann English Language Teaching. This sheet may be photocopied and used within the class.

12

Personal Information Sheet

Aim

To help students get to know each other.

Language

What's your name?

Where's your hometown?

Tell me about your family.

What are your hobbies? etc.

Preparation

This is useful with a new class. Also it's a good reference to keep on hand as everyone gets to know each other better.

Copy Worksheet 12.

Procedure

1. In class, hand out the worksheet to every student and put them into pairs.

2. Have them interview each other and write their partner's information on the new sheet. Students may need some coaching on how to phrase the questions, so go through each item and demonstrate the appropriate questions. For example, *What's your name? Where's your hometown? Tell me about your family. What are your hobbies/interests? What travel experience do you have? Why do you study English? What do you want to do in the future?*

3. In addition, encourage students to ask one more question of their own design.

4. Put two pairs of students together and have students introduce their partners to the other pair. Encourage students to ask at least one follow-up question for every item on the paper.

Variations

1. Rather than having pairs introduce themselves, have one student introduce his/her partner to the whole class.

2. Have students introduce each other to the rest of the class by swapping papers.

3. When students have finished, collect all of the original papers. Randomly pick one paper out of the stack and begin reading pieces of information. Other students try to guess whose paper it is. (Of course, students and their partners should feign ignorance when their papers are read.)

4. Make a teacher's copy of everyone's worksheet and at a point later in the year, quiz the class to see how much they remember about each other.

5. Have students fill in the worksheet prior to the next class.

Further Practice

As a review or practice of the language elements in this lesson, at a later date, give each student another copy of the worksheet and also give each student one of the *Who am I?* cards (Worksheets 6a and 6b). Follow the teacher's notes for *Who am I?*, but this time students will need to write down the information.

Personal Information Sheet

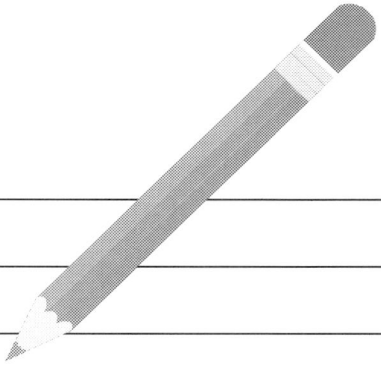

Name: _____

Hometown: _____

Family members: _____

_____

_____

_____

_____

Hobbies/Interests:

1. _____

2. _____

3. _____

4. _____

Travel experience: _____

_____

_____

Reason(s) for studying English: _____

_____

_____

In the future: _____

_____

Other information: _____

_____

©North Star Publishing Co. 1995
Published by Heinemann English Language Teaching. This sheet may be photocopied and used within the class.

Password

Aim

To reinforce knowledge of simple items of vocabulary.

Language

Vocabulary of common objects and descriptive terms

Preparation

Copy Worksheets 13a–d and cut into cards before class. Demonstrate how to do this activity by picking one of the cards from the stack and offering one-word hints until someone has guessed the right password. Show the card to the class.

Procedure

1. Divide the class into two teams.

2. Explain the two rules. First, gestures, body language and other hints such as squeals or grunts are not permitted. Second, students may not use part of the answer in the hint, for example, *book* for *notebook* results in a lost turn.

3. One person from each team comes to the front of the class. Show the first password card to both students.

4. Students take turns giving a one-word hint to their respective teams until the correct password has been identified.

5. When the correct answer has been given, two new students come forward. Continue to the end of the stack.

Scoring: Correct answer given after first hint = 4 points, second = 3 points, third = 2 points and the final hint = 1 point.

Variations

1. Lower-level students may use a sentence, phrase or clause as a hint rather than a single word.

2. Start the scoring higher to allow more chances, especially with lower-level students.

3. Try making all of the hints gestures only, "Charade-style." The answers must be, of course, verbal.

Further Practice

When finished, put students into groups of two or three. Give each group four or five cards to see if they can put them into a sentence or story. These should be read to the class.

Password

airplane	ant	apple	bag
banana	bank	baseball	beach
belt	bicycle	bird	boat
book	boss	bowl	box
bracelet	bread	bus	button
calendar	camera	car	cat
chair	chicken	cloud	coffee
coin	comb	computer	cookie

©North Star Publishing Co. 1995
Published by Heinemann English Language Teaching. This sheet may be photocopied and used within the class.

Password

cow	cup	dictionary	dog
door	earring	egg 	elephant
elevator	eraser	fan	fish 
flower 	garage	garden	glasses
guitar 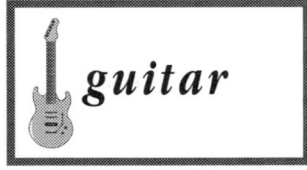	hat	heart	hill
hospital	hotel	house 	ice
key 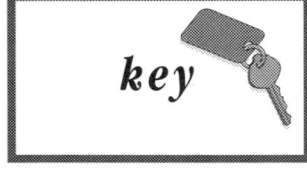	knife	lamp	letter
library	magazine	mailbox	match 

©North Star Publishing Co. 1995
Published by Heinemann English Language Teaching. This sheet may be photocopied and used within the class.

Password

milk	money	moon	mountain
mouse	necklace	newspaper	nose
ocean	orange	pencil	pepper
piano	picture	pillow	plate
plum	pocket	rabbit	radio
rain	refrigerator	ring	river
rock	ruler	salt	sandwich
school	scissors	shirt	shoe

©North Star Publishing Co. 1995
Published by Heinemann English Language Teaching. This sheet may be photocopied and used within the class.

Password

shower	snake	snow	soap
socks	sofa	spoon	stamp
star	street	sun	table
taxi	teacher	telephone	television
toaster	tomato	toothbrush	towel
train	tree	truck	umbrella
violin	wallet	wastebasket	watch
water	wind	window	

©North Star Publishing Co. 1995
Published by Heinemann English Language Teaching. This sheet may be photocopied and used within the class.

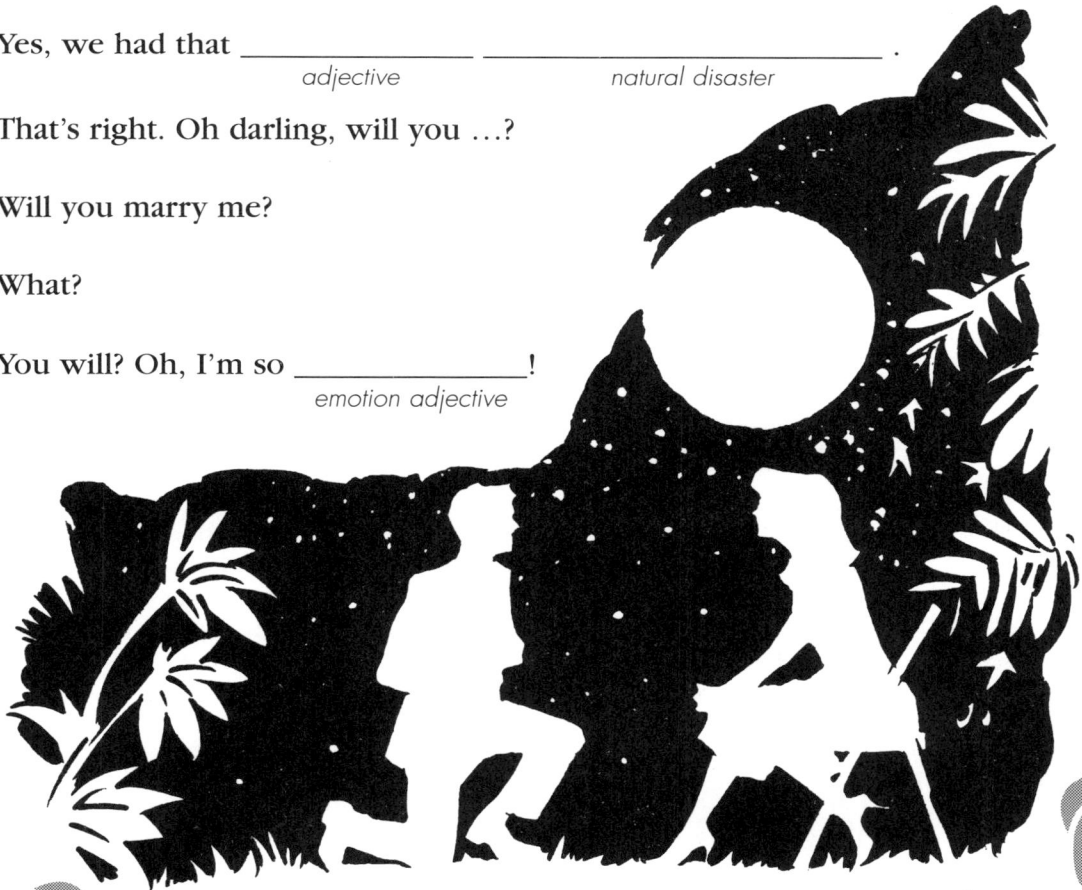

The Proposal
Young Man

1. My little _____ , have I ever told you how much I love you?
dessert

3. I have a very _____ question to ask you.
adjective

5. Will you…? Will you…?

7. _____ heart, you know, we've been dating for _____ years now.
Taste adjective   *number*

9. Do you remember our first date?

11. Didn't we _____ all evening?
sports verb

13. Yes. That's when I fell in love with you.

15. Yes, we had that _____ _____ .
adjective   *natural disaster*

17. That's right. Oh darling, will you …?

19. Will you marry me?

21. What?

23. You will? Oh, I'm so _____!
emotion adjective

14 The Proposal

Aim

To expand vocabulary.

To identify parts of speech and to distinguish non-count from singular and plural count nouns.

Language

Everyday nouns and adjectives

Preparation

This is a very simple and enjoyable activity for vocabulary growth in addition to practicing singular and plural noun forms, spelling and fundamental parts of speech. Pre-teach the required language by writing phrases such as the following on the board: *Give me the name of a vegetable*, *Name an insect*, *Tell me an emotion adjective*, etc. Have students call out three or four items for each phrase and write these on the board as well. Review non-count and count nouns as well as singular and plural forms.

Also, make sure that students know the meaning of the words *adjective*, *emotion*, *natural disaster*, and *expression of anger*.

Copy Worksheets 14a and 14b prior to class.

Procedure

1. Pair the students and hand out the worksheets, one to Student A and the other to Student B.

2. Have students ask their partners for the appropriate information to fill in the blanks.

3. When both have asked for and received this information, have them read their script by alternating lines, i.e., Student A begins by reading Line 1 on his/her page. Student B responds by reading Line 2 from his/her page. Students will be amused by this (not so?) romantic proposal.

Variations

1. Have pairs of students read their scripts to the rest of the class.

2. Encourage students to perform their scenes in front of the rest of the class.

3. Have all of the A students remain in their seats and rotate the B students one to the right. This way, new pairs are formed. Have them read through *The Proposal* again.

4. Have pairs of students write down only the words that were used to fill in the blanks. Using this list, have them compose a completely different story, using the words in order from their answer sheets.

Further Practice

Even though this acitivity is pretty silly, it is a good lead-in to a discussion about proposing – a custom that often varies from culture to culture. If the class is composed of mostly single students, have them discuss what they think a culturally-appropriate proposal would be. Perhaps students could roleplay in front of the class. If the class is primarily made up of married students, discuss their own proposal experiences.

The Proposal
Young Woman

2. Yes, my little _____. And I love you too.
animal

4. Oh? What is it?

6. Come on. What is it my little _____?
fruit

8. Really, I thought it was _____ years.
number

10. I'll never forget. We went to the _____.
public place

12. Yes, and after that didn't we _____ till morning?
party verb

14. And do you remember when we went to _____?
faraway place

16. I remember. That was the first time you touched my _____.
part of the body

18. I don't have all day! What is it?

20. _____ !?
Expression of anger

22. Just kidding. Of course, you silly little _____ . I'll marry you.
vegetable

24. Me too.

©North Star Publishing Co. 1995
Published by Heinemann English Language Teaching. This sheet may be photocopied and used within the class.

15

Strip Quiz 2

Aim

To encourage students to tell a story by ordering sentences.

Language

Simple narrative in the past tense

Preparation

Prior to class, copy Worksheet 15 and cut into strips.

Markers are words that are used to signal sequential order and transition within a story. Students usually have little trouble organizing the parts of this story, but sometimes they need help in understanding which words controlled their choice. In class, before beginning this activity, identify some markers for them and demonstrate their use.

Procedure

1. Divide the class into groups of seven and hand out the strips of paper. (If a small class, give some of the students two strips each.)

2. Without looking at each other's papers, the students should read their own strip(s) out at random and then discuss the order together until all the strips of paper are organized into the correct order.

3. When they have finished, explain that the story is actually a quiz.

Answer

The doctor is the boy's mother.

Variations

1. Have students stand in the correct order.

2. Have students memorize their strips.

Further Practice

1. See *Strip Quiz* 1 (Worksheet 8).

2. Discuss the cultural reasons behind the assumption that doctors have traditionally been thought of as being male. Are these assumptions changing? Challenge students to think of other occupations that are traditionally associated with one sex or the other.

Strip Quiz 2
The Doctor

A father and his son were driving on the highway. They had a terrible accident.

The father was killed instantly and the son was injured.

The son was taken to a hospital by ambulance.

At the hospital a doctor walked into the operating room.

The doctor looked at the boy and said:

"Oh no! This boy is my son!"

How was this possible?

16 Phrases and Places

Aim

To familiarize students with commonly heard phrases which they might not otherwise have studied.

Language

A variety of polite statements, requests, instructions, enquiries, etc., used to carry out transactions in public places

Preparation

These common phrases are frequently used in easily identifiable places. See if students can match the phrases with the correct places. Often, when students travel abroad, they return feeling quite perplexed because the English they heard on their trip is different from what they studied. This lesson introduces ordinary colloquial English that may come in handy someday.

Procedure

1. Copy and hand out Worksheet 16 to all the students and have them cover the phrases and look only at the places.

2. Read down the list to check for understanding.

3. Then have students cover the places column and look only at the phrases. Again check for understanding.

4. Starting with the first phrase: *Turn to page 109*, see how many students can identify the correct place where this phrase would be heard.

Variations

1. Don't hand out the copies at first; instead, use this as a listening exercise.

2. Divide the class into teams and have them compete against each other to be the first to identify the correct place.

3. Do this as a pairwork activity by having the students fold their copies vertically thus dividing the phrases from the places.

4. To develop communication skills, have students offer appropriate responses to the phrases, for example *Is that for one night or two? Two, please.* The conversation could continue as a roleplay at a hotel to discuss the kind of room (single, twin, double, suite), the price, the method of payment (cash, credit card, etc.).

5. During or after the exercise, make a list of unfamiliar words on the board.

Further Practice

Have groups of students create mini-dramas which include one of the phrases. They should write a dialogue to go before and after the assigned phrase. Have students then act out their mini-dramas before the rest of the class.

Answers

1C, 2M, 3L, 4B, 5I, 6S, 7G, 8A, 9P, 10F, 11N, 12H, 13R, 14T, 15Q, 16D, 17O, 18J, 19K, 20E

Note Some phrases could be associated with more than one place.

Phrases and Places

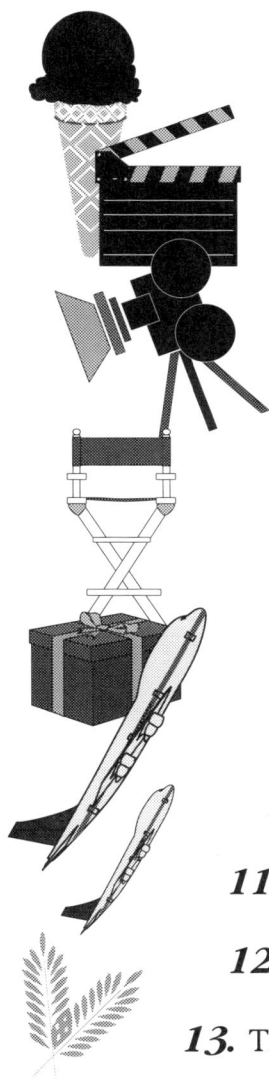

1. Turn to page 109.

2. Don't feed the bears.

3. Single or double dip?

4. A double, on the rocks.

5. Want me to fill her up?

6. Lights! Camera! Action!

7. Is that for one night or two?

8. Our Sunday Brunch is $9.95.

9. Take four of these, twice a day.

10. What size prints do you want?

11. Quiet, please. People are reading.

12. Would you like this gift-wrapped?

13. This should take about a week by air.

14. May I see your boarding pass, please?

15. Occasional showers throughout the day.

16. Let's see, you want a dozen cream-filled?

17. Would you like to open a savings account?

18. The wheat will be ready for harvest this week.

19. On your left you can see the Statue of Liberty.

20. Wow! I don't believe it. Two strikes and a spare.

a. restaurant

b. bar

c. classroom

d. donut shop

e. bowling alley

f. photo shop

g. hotel

h. department store

i. gas station

j. farm

k. New York tour bus

l. ice-cream shop

m. zoo

n. library

o. bank

p. doctor's office

q. weather report

r. post office

s. movie studio

t. airport

©North Star Publishing Co. 1995
Published by Heinemann English Language Teaching. This sheet may be photocopied and used within the class.

Gracie and Gus Go Shopping

Aim

To practice words and phrases commonly used in a large department store.

Language

Questions and statements about goods and services available in a large store

Preparation

Students can do this activity in pairs or in fours, sixes or eights. Copy the route-cards (Worksheets 17a and 17b), one for each pair or group, and copy the response sheets (Worksheets 17c and 17d) for half the number of students taking part.

The response sheets are clearly divided into sections A–F which correspond directly to the sections on the route cards. Each student will either read the questions on the route cards (i.e., as the customer) or the responses (i.e., as the sales people).

Each group will need a die and each pair of students will need some kind of marker such as a coin, eraser or token: these should be prepared prior to the beginning of class.

Procedure

1. Hand out either one or both of the route-cards depending on the amount of time available. (One worksheet will require about twenty-five minutes.)

2. Pair the students into teams, then put two, three or four pairs together. Pairs will compete against each other to be the first to reach the end of the route-cards.

3. The first pair begins by one player rolling a die, moving the appropriate number of spaces and reading the question. His/Her partner searches through the sentences on the response sheet and offers a reply. (There is only one appropriate response for each question.) After a response has been given (and the others in the group consent that the response was appropriate), the next pair takes its turn. If another pair's marker is on the square they should move to, they must roll again.

Variations

1. For more advanced students, after landing on a square and correctly matching the questions with the response, have the player roll the die again. Have two students role-play a conversation about the square's topic which extends to the number of sentences equal to the number rolled, for example, three sentences.

2. To make the activity more difficult, add time limits, penalties for incorrect responses (for example: loss of turn, go back three squares), coffee breaks, etc.

3. Don't hand out the response sheets. Instead, have students create their own responses.

Start

These gloves cost $17.51. Here's $20.00.

I'm looking for a birthday present for my brother.

Is there a bank in this store?

Where's the music department?

Can I try this sweater on?

How do I get to the coffee shop?

Could you tell me where the toy department is?

Do you think this tie goes with this jacket?

Excuse me, where can I buy some socks?

A

B

How much does this cost?

Can I get a key made here?

Do you accept travelers checks?

Do you sell perfume?

What sizes do you have?

Is this on sale too?

Could you tell me where the restrooms are?

Is there a drinking fountain nearby?

Could you tell me the time?

I think my watch needs a new battery.

B

C

Do you have these shoes in a larger size?

Do you have this in another color?

Where can I get my parking ticket stamped?

I'm looking for a desk.

Does Frank Jones work here?

Could you tell me where the public telephones are?

How much are these books?

This camera doesn't work. Can I exchange it?

This T-shirt is too small. Do you have a larger one?

When is the sale over?

SALE

C

C

D

Would you gift wrap this please?

I can't find my sister! Who should I talk to?

Does this sale include order-made suits?

Do you take credit cards?

Are you open on Sundays?

HOURS OF OPENING

Where can I throw this away?

D

OPEN

What time do you close?

I'd like one of those, please. Could you put it in a bag?

Excuse me, is there a restaurant in the store?

Do you have anything cheaper?

E

Do you deliver?

Is there a travel agency in the store?

Hmm...that's expensive, isn't it?

Can I get a refund on this shirt?

Could I have change for a dollar, please?

I've lost my wallet!

Where can I mail this letter?

What time do you open tomorrow?

How long will it take to re-string my tennis racket?

Is this made of leather or plastic?

E

F

How long will it take to process this roll of film?

Does that price include tax?

Gifts

Can I buy a gift certificate here?

Is this coupon still good?

Where's the ice-cream shop?

Finish

I'd like to apply for a job. Who should I talk to?

Could you tell me where the pet shop is?

How does this microwave oven work?

Do you have another set like this one?

GRACIE AND GUS GO SHOPPING

A

"Sure, there's a dressing room over there."
"Thank you. Here's your change: $2.49."
"Yes, there's a bank on the first floor across from the florist."
"Socks can be found on the fourth floor next to the Sports Department."
"How old is your brother?"
"I think the blue tie goes better with that jacket?"
"The Toy Department is on the third floor."
"The Music Department is next to the Electrical Department on the 2nd floor."
"Go straight to the Jewelry Department and turn left. The coffee shop is on the right."

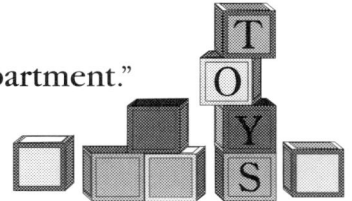

B

"The restrooms are on the 6th floor."
"Sure, please show me your passport."
"They are $25.00 each."
"Here, let me take a look at it."
"No, I'm sorry. That's not on sale this week."
"We sell many kinds of perfume from all over the world."
"We have sizes from 8 to 18."
"No, you can't get a key made here. Try the hardware store across the street."
"It's a quarter after four."
"Sure, there's a drinking fountain next to the elevator."

C

"Sorry, we only have orange and purple."
"Have it stamped at the customer service desk on your way out."
"They cost $10.95 each."
"Try the Furniture Department on the 3rd floor."
"Please ask at the Information Desk."
"The sale will continue until Saturday."
"We only have that style of shoe in smaller sizes, I'm afraid."
"I'm sorry, we don't. But I can order one from our main branch."
"You can exchange the camera if you have a receipt."
"Public telephones are on the first floor near the information desk."

Published by Heinemann English Language Teaching. This sheet may be photocopied and used within the class.

PHOTOCOPIABLE

GRACIE AND GUS GO SHOPPING

D

"Yes, we're open from Monday to Sunday."
"What color paper would you like?"
"I'm afraid not."
"There's a trash can next to the escalator."
"I'm sorry, that is the cheapest one we have."
"Have you gone to the Lost and Found Department?"
"We take Visa, Master Card and American Express."
"We close at 5:30 p.m."
"There are many restaurants on the top floor."
"Yes, I can put it in a bag for you."

E

"Yes, World's Best Travel is on the 7th floor."
"I'm sorry but we don't give refunds."
"Yes, it's one of the more expensive brands."
"Yes, we deliver from Monday through Friday."
"Sure, here's two quarters, three dimes, and four nickels."
"It's genuine cow leather."
"About two hours."
"There's a mailbox just in front of this store."
"We open at 9:00 a.m. sharp."
"Have you gone to the Lost and Found Department?"

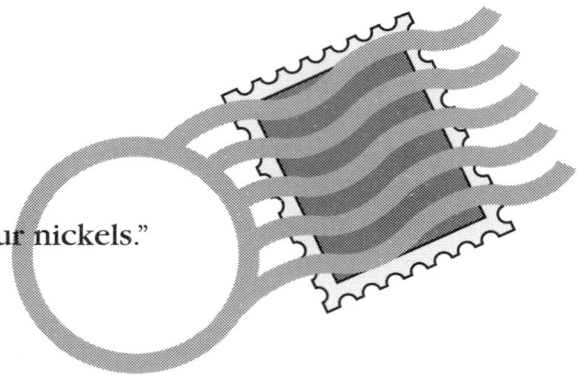

F

"Yes, it's good until Friday."
"The pet shop is in the basement."
"No, the tax isn't included."
"Sure, we have them in values of ten, twenty, or fifty dollars."
"See that sign? No Smoking!"
"No, I'm sorry. That's the last one we have."
"It will be ready in an hour."
"You can apply for a job at the Personnel Department."
"Here's the on/off switch and here's the timer."

©North Star Publishing Co. 1995
Published by Heinemann English Language Teaching. This sheet may be photocopied and used within the class.

Can you ....?

How well can you ...?

	YES/NO (Y or N)	I'm an excellent	I	I	I'm an average	I'm not a good	I	YES/NO (Y or N)	I'm an excellent	I	I	I'm an average	I'm not a good	I
		Student 1 — well. — pretty well. — — — poorly/badly.							Student 2 — well. — pretty well. — — — poorly/badly.					
1. Can you ice-skate? (skater)														
2. Can you play the piano? (pianist)														
3. Can you dance? (dancer)														
4. Can you run? (runner/athlete)														
5. Can you play ping-pong? (player)														
6. Can you speak English? (English speaker)														
7. Can you swim? (swimmer)														
8. Can you cook? (cook/chef)														
9. Can you play the guitar? (guitarist)														
10. Can you ski? (skier)														
11. Can you paint a picture? (artist)														
12. Can you type? (typist)														
13. Can you ride a horse? (rider)														
14. Can you _____? (_____)														

PHOTOCOPIABLE

Can you ...?

Aim

To talk to other students about skills and varying levels of ability.

Language

Can you ...?
How well can you ... ?
I'm (not) a good ...
I'm an average/excellent ...
I ... (pretty) badly/well.

Preparation

This very versatile exercise is for the purpose of talking about people's abilities. Before handing out the worksheet, on the board write all of the response patterns to be used, e.g., *I'm an excellent _____, I _____ well, I _____ pretty well*, etc. Explain the usage of both the noun form (*I'm not a good dancer*) and the verb form (*I dance pretty well*). Select students at random to participate in a demonstration conversation, answering some model questions in complete sentences.

This pairwork activity actually has two parts. The first is the simple *Can you ...?* question which requires only a *Yes* or *No* answer. Explain that *Yes* means that the speaker has the ability to do the task, even if he or she is not good at it. *No* means that the task is completely beyond his/her ability. If a *Yes* answer is given, continue on to the second part of the question, i.e., *How well can you ...?* If a *No* answer is given, do not continue to the second part of the question.

Prior to class copy Worksheets 18a and 18b.

Procedure

1. Pair the students and hand out Worksheets a and b to each of the two students respectively.

2. Students should write their partner's name on the line titled Student 1. (The column for Student 2 comes later.)

3. One student begins asking a *Can you ... ?* question to his/her partner. The response is written in the appropiate box on the left of Student 1 column.

4. If the response is *Yes*, the same student asks *How well can you ... ?* The response is appropriately marked under the Student 1 column.

5. Have pairs go through the thirteen questions and add one final *Can you ...?* question of their own design.

6. When pairs have finished, separate them and form new pairs. Have students write the name of their new partner's former partner on the line titled Student 2. This time they will be asking about their new partner's first partner using the third person. Questions should be changed from *Can you ...?* to *Can he/she ...?*

Variations

1. Use the *Student 1* column for guessing the partners' answers before the questions are asked. Then pair the students and have them use the *Student 2* column for actual answers.

2. Use as a *Crossfire* exercise with paired partners sitting in groups of four as if at a card table. Partners sit diagonal to each other. Dictation takes place simultaneously with the two teams competing to be heard over their competitors and racing to the finish.

3. Introduce the *How often do you ...?* pattern for follow-up questioning.

Further Practice

See *Find Someone Who ...* (Worksheet 9), *Likes and Dislikes* (Worksheets 5a and 5b), *When was the first time you ...?* (Worksheets 28a and 28b), *When was the last time you ...?* (Worksheets 22a and 22b).

Can you ....?

How well can you ...?

	YES/NO (Y or N)	I'm an excellent	I _____ well.	I _____ pretty well.	I'm an average	I'm not a good	I _____ poorly.	YES/NO (Y or N)	I'm an excellent	I _____ well.	I _____ pretty well.	I'm an average	I'm not a good	I _____ poorly.
		Student 1							**Student 2**					
1. Can you surf? (surfer)														
2. Can you sing? (singer)														
3. Can you play tennis? (tennis-player)														
4. Can you play the violin? (violinist)														
5. Can you write a story? (writer)														
6. Can you fish? (fisherman)														
7. Can you juggle? (juggler)														
8. Can you act? (actor/actress)														
9. Can you fix a flat tire? (mechanic)														
10. Can you grow vegetables? (gardener)														
11. Can you climb a mountain? (climber)														
12. Can you drive a car? (driver)														
13. Can you play golf? (golfer)														
14. Can you _____? (_____)														

19

Opposites 2

Aim

To expand students' active knowledge of adjectives.

Language

60 adjectives

Preparation

This list of opposites includes common adjectives. It is especially intended for beginning students and is a great pairwork or whole class confidence builder. To establish a stronger vocabulary base, students can usually attach *not* to most of these words, thus doubling their ability to have a conversation. For example, if a student does not know the opposite of *happy*, there is always the safe description that something is *not happy*. The subtlety between *happy* and *not happy* probably is not terrifically important among beginning students.

Procedure

1. Give each student in class a copy of Worksheet 19.

2. Start by going down the list to check for understanding by saying the word and asking for synonyms or examples of its meaning. Students will need to know the meanings of all the words before they can proceed with this lesson.

3. Next, divide the class into two or three groups. Read the first word off the list. Whichever group supplies an appropriate opposite gets a point. The group with the most points at the end is the winner. For higher level classes, students must put the opposite word in a sentence to get a point.

Variations

1. Use these words for *Password* (Worksheets 13a–d) once students have learned them.

2. For listening practice, do the lesson without handing out the paper first.

3. As a pairwork activity, have one student cover up the right list and the other the left.

4. Encourage students to make sentences using opposites, e.g. *Yesterday I was happy but today I am sad.*

Further Practice

1. Pair students and have them compose sentences using two (or three) of the listed words in a single sentence. For example *Everyone was happy that the warm picnic was the first one of the year.* Have pairs swap their sentences and write opposite sentences: *Everyone was sad that the cool picnic was the last one of the year.*

2. As a writing exercise, have pairs of students compose a short story using either the left or right column of words.

3. Time the class to see how quickly they can go through the entire opposites list – without their papers. Make a note of the time and review the list occasionally, each time trying to reduce the time. With enough practice, students should be able to complete the list in under a minute.

Answers

happy – sad	bright – dark/dull	different – same
warm – cool	quiet – noisy	sharp – dull
heavy – light	soft – hard	upper – lower
wrong – right	more – less	terrible – wonderful
hungry – full	true – false	adult – child
expensive – cheap	strong – weak	deep – shallow
top – bottom	wide – narrow	wise – foolish
smooth – rough	tight – loose	tired – rested/refreshed
tall – short	safe – dangerous	used – new
strange – normal	interesting – boring	future – past

Opposites 2

happy	*sad*	strong	
warm		wide	
heavy		tight	
wrong		safe	
hungry		interesting	
expensive		different	
top		sharp	
smooth		upper	
tall		terrible	
strange		adult	
bright		deep	
quiet		wise	
soft		tired	
more		used	
true		future	

©North Star Publishing Co. 1995
Published by Heinemann English Language Teaching. This sheet may be photocopied and used within the class.

20 Tic Tac Toe 2

Aim To practice asking tag questions.

Language All forms of tags, e.g. *isn't he, aren't you, haven't they, won't we, didn't I*, etc.

Preparation This lesson reinforces students' knowledge and use of tag questions in a fun and competitive way.

Play a few games of regular nine-square Tic Tac Toe. Number the squares so that the students can identify the square of their choice by stating the number. Once students are familiar with the game, expand the number of squares to a grid containing 20 squares (see the worksheet). Pair or group the students and set up a mark for each, e.g. square, circle, triangle, star, etc. Draw these marks somewhere on the board.

The object of the game is to place three of the same marks in a continuous line either horizontally, vertically or diagonally. Copy Worksheet 20, hand out and explain the rules.

Procedure 1. The starting team must ask a question to another team in the class. To be able to have its mark placed in one of the squares, the team must use correct English or no mark will be given. A minimum five-word question is suggested.

2. If the asking team's question uses correct English, the designated defending team must answer. An answer that is given in the wrong tense or uses incorrect English results in the loss of a turn. (The defending team does not get a mark regardless of the answer; only the questioning team has a chance for a mark.)

3. Rotate among the teams so each team, in turn, asks a question to another.

4. It may be best to determine a time limit (about 30 or 45 seconds) for composing questions and answers to keep the lesson active.

Variations After a dozen rounds or so, the grid becomes pretty full of marks which makes winning very difficult. Explain that one team can challenge the mark of another team by asking a question. The rules are as follows:

1. If the challenging team's question uses correct English and the defending team's answer is also correct English, there is no change. For example, Team Y wants its mark on Square 13 where Team X already has its mark. In this case, Team Y challenges Team X by asking a tag question, e.g., *George Washington had wooden teeth, didn't he?* If Team X replies *Yes, he did*, the challenge fails and there are no changes.

2. If the challenging team's question uses correct English but the answer is grammatically or factually incorrect, the defending team will lose one of its marks as decided by the challenging team. For example, Team Y asks *George Washington had wooden teeth, didn't he?* If Team X responds with *Yes, he is* or *No, he had <u>stainless steel</u> teeth*, the mark is removed. (Note: Team Y cannot put its mark in the square; the space has only been cleared.)

3. If the challenging team's question uses incorrect English, the defending team need not answer. For example, *George Washington had wooden teeth, isn't he?* In this case, Team X need not respond.

Further Practice 1. Have students write four or five complete questions by assigning them the horizontal or vertical rows, respectively. Later, pair the students and have them exchange papers and discuss or write out the answers to the questions.

2. Pick any four or five question starters from the grid and write them on the board. Have all of the students complete the questions.

3. See *Tic Tac Toe* 1 (Worksheet 10).

Tic Tac Toe 2

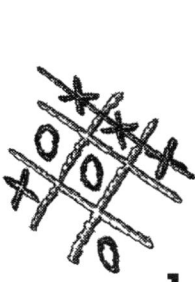     

1.

…, didn't he?

2.

…, aren't they?

3.

…, won't we?

4.

…, couldn't you?

5.

…, shouldn't we?

6.

…, can't you?

7.

…, doesn't she?

8.

…, won't it?

9.

…, didn't they?

10.

…, hasn't she?

11.

…, weren't you?

12.

…, wasn't I?

13.

…, don't they?

14.

…, isn't she?

15.

…, haven't we?

16.

…, didn't it?

17.

…, aren't you?

18.

…, doesn't he?

19.

…, can't she?

20.

…, couldn't they?

21 The Alien

Aim

To practice asking simple questions.

Language

Is he/she/it ...?

What ...?

How old ...?

Does he/she/it ...?

Preparation

This activity is good for helping beginning students learn how to formulate basic questions and responses. Demonstrate on the board by drawing an alien. Encourage students to ask questions such as *Is it male or female? What is his/her name? What color is his/her hair?* etc. Write a few of these on the board and help students write complete sentence answers next to each. Encourage students to ask additional questions such as *Is he/she noisy or quiet? How old is he/she? What color are his/her eyes?* etc.

During the questioning, demonstrate how to use negative responses such as *He doesn't have any hair, She doesn't have any fingers* and *It doesn't have a spaceship.*

Procedure

1. Begin the activity with a story like this: *You have recently returned from a one-year trip through the galaxy. On the way you were introduced to many different aliens and cultures. You became friends with some of them and one in particular became a close friend.*

2. At this point, hand out Worksheet 21 to the students and have them draw a picture of their alien friend in the box in the center. Remind students to include their friend's name and sex above their picture. Then have them fill in the information under the *My Friend* column. Students should think of two additional questions and write these on the appropriate lines at the bottom of the question list. Allow two or three minutes.

3. Then pair the students and have them ask each other the questions as printed on the page. The responses to the questions should be written in the *Partner's Answers* column.

Variations

1. Write additional questions on the board to stimulate further discussion, for example *What is his/her favorite food? What did you talk about with him/her? What is his/her job*, etc.

2. Put students into groups of three. Have them draw their alien friend, then, interview-style, Student A asks Student B about Student C's alien. For example, Student A asks *Is it male or female?* Student B says *I don't know* or *I'm not sure.* Then Student B asks Student C *Is it male or female?* Student C replies *She's female.* Student B relates this information back to Student A who writes the information in the *Partner's Answers* column.

3. Have students assume the role of the alien and do this lesson about their human friend. In pairs, students draw their partner's picture and answer the questions according to their partner's information.

Further Practice

Have students write a one-week diary of their visit to the alien's planet as a writing assignment.

In pairs or small groups, have students plan for a home-stay visit to Earth by their alien friend.

21

The ALIEN

Friend's name: _____

Sex: _____

My *friend*

Questions:

Is it male or female?

What's his/her name?

Where is he/she from?

How old is he/she?

What does he/she do?

Is he/she married?

Does he/she have kids?

What does he/she eat?

What does he/she drink?

When does he/she sleep?

What color is his/her hair?

What color is his/her _____?

What color are his/her eyes?

What color are his/her _____?

What languages does he/she speak?

What is his/her hobby?

_____?

_____?

Answers:

He/She is _____

His/Her name is _____

He/She is from _____

He/She is _____ years old.

He/She is a(n) _____

_____, he/she is/isn't.

_____, he/she does/doesn't.

He/She eats _____.

He/She drinks _____.

He/She sleeps at/in _____.

His/Her hair is _____.

His/Her _____ is _____.

His/Her eyes are _____.

His/Her _____ are _____.

He/She speaks _____

and _____.

His/Her hobby is _____.

_____.

_____.

He/She doesn't sleep.

Partner's answers:

He/She is _____

His/Her name is _____

He/She is from _____

He/She is _____ years old.

He/She is a(n) _____

_____, he/she is/isn't.

_____, he/she does/doesn't.

He/She eats _____.

He/She drinks _____.

He/She sleeps at/in _____.

His/Her hair is _____.

His/Her _____ is _____.

His/Her eyes are _____.

His/Her _____ are _____.

He/She speaks _____

and _____.

His/Her hobby is _____.

_____.

_____.

He/She doesn't have a/an/

any _____.

PHOTOCOPIABLE

When was the last time you ...?

Aim

To use the simple past tense together with specific time expressions.

Language

last night/day/week/month/year

x days/weeks/months/years ago

the day before yesterday

the night/week/month/year before last

Preparation

This pairwork exercise is useful for practicing the simple past tense and specific time expressions. Carefully explain and demonstrate the specific time expressions by writing them on the board. Point out that it is often possible to refer to a time in two or three ways. For example, if today is Monday, *last Saturday* would be the same as *two days ago* or *the day before yesterday*.

Before beginning this exercise, review the following: *Last night/week/month/year/Wednesday/June*, etc.; *two days ago, three weeks ago, four months ago*, etc.; *the day before yesterday*; the *night/week/month before last*, etc. Point out that *ago* is used with numbers and *the night before last* means *the night before last night*. Finally, negative responses should also be written on the board such as *I don't/can't remember, I forget, Never, I never ...* .

Note Common responses such as *yesterday* and *this morning* are intentionally omitted so that students can practice other, less frequently used specific expressions of time.

Procedure

1. Pair the students and hand out Worksheets 22a and 22b, one to each student respectively.

2. Have them ask each other the *When was the last time you ...?* questions and write their partner's responses in the appropriate spaces. They should fill in one of the columns in any one line, but they could then be encouraged to fill in two or all three. Finally, ask students to think of one additional question for line 13.

Variations

1. For higher-level students, encourage the use of follow-up questions. *When was the last time you played tennis? Where did you play? Who did you play with? Did you win? How often do you play? Who is your favorite tennis player?* etc.

2. Use as a *Crossfire* exercise with paired partners sitting in groups of four as if at a card table. Partners sit diagonal to each other. Questions are asked simultaneously with the two teams competing to be heard over their competitors and racing to the finish.

Further Practice

1. See *When was the first time you ...?* (Worksheets 28a and 28b)

2. Using the pattern *When was the last time you ...?* have students refer to *Can you ...?* (Worksheets 18a and 18b).

A

22a

SPECIFIC TIME EXPRESSIONS

The day before yesterday. The night before last (night). The week before last (week). The month before last (month). The year before last (year).												

Two days ago. Three weeks ago. Four weekends ago. Five months ago. Six years ago.												

Last night. Last Sunday. Last week. Last month. Last year.												

When was the last time you ...?

1. ... fried an egg?
2. ... went to a movie theater?
3. ... took a trip?
4. ... ate a pizza?
5. ... visited a friend in hospital?
6. ... went to a disco?
7. ... received a letter?
8. ... talked to a dog?
9. ... fell asleep while reading?
10. ... went to zoo?
11. ... had a nightmare/bad dream?
12. ... broke something?
13. ...   ?

B

SPECIFIC TIME EXPRESSIONS

	Last night. Last Sunday. Last week. Last month. Last year.	Two days ago. Three weeks ago. Four weekends ago. Five months ago. Six years ago.	The day before yesterday. The night before last (night). The week before last (week). The month before last (month). The year before last (year).

When was the last time you ...?

1. ... read a book?
2. ... played cards?
3. ... took a photograph?
4. ... wrote a letter?
5. ... ate breakfast in a restaurant?
6. ... held hands with someone?
7. ... went to the dentist?
8. ... used a screwdriver?
9. ... had a haircut?
10. ... gave someone flowers?
11. ... told a lie?
12. ... made a long-distance phone call?
13. ... _____?

©North Star Publishing Co. 1995
Published by Heinemann English Language Teaching. This sheet may be photocopied and used within the class.

"A kind of" Crossword Puzzle

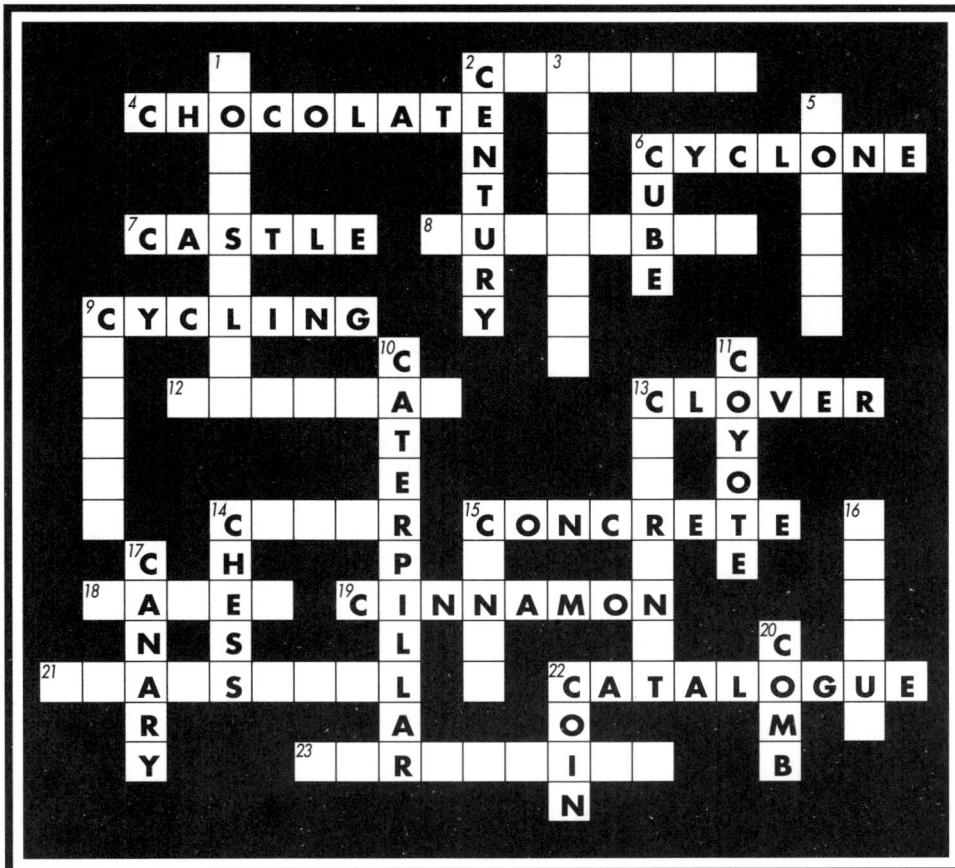

Across

4. A kind of sweet; it's brown
6. A kind of storm; it's dangerous
7. A kind of house; it's old
9. A kind of sport; it's fast
13. A kind of plant; it has three leaves
15. A kind of building material; it's hard
19. A kind of spice; it's brown
22. A kind of magazine; it's free

Down

2. A kind of time unit; it's very long
6. A kind of shape; it has six sides
10. A kind of insect; it's hairy
11. A kind of animal; it howls
14. A kind of game; it's difficult
17. A kind of bird; it sings
20. A kind of tool; it has teeth
22. A kind of money; it's metal

Helpful Language

What's number ___ across / down?

Give me another hint, (please).

What's the 2nd (3rd, 4th, 5th, 6th, 7th, 8th, 9th) letter?

How do you spell _____ ?

©North Star Publishing Co. 1995
Published by Heinemann English Language Teaching. This sheet may be photocopied and used within the class.

23

"A kind of" Crossword Puzzle

Aim

To practice listening and spelling and ask for hints.

Language

30 words beginning with *C*

Preparation

This activity focuses on listening as well as spelling skills. All of the answers represent *a kind of* something and they all begin with the letter *C* to limit the number of choices. Many of the answers included in the puzzle have tricky spellings so students will need to help each other by asking for hints, first for the answers themselves, and then also for the spelling. Review the helpful language at the bottom of the worksheet, especially *What's the second, third, last*, etc. *letter?*

It may be helpful to write the questions *Would you read number 1 again, please?* and *How do you spell x?* on the board.

Copy Worksheets 23a and 23b prior to class.

Procedure

1. Pair the students and hand out parts A and B. Explain that the two hints given on each page are to be given one at a time to their partner. If further hints are required, they will need to be supplied from their partner.

2. Have the students ask each other in turn for a hint for each word. The first pair to complete their puzzle wins.

Variations

1. Encourage students to create their own hints rather than read the ones provided.

2. Prior to making copies, white out all of the answers and copy the hints for both A and B. In this way, the blank puzzle can be done individually in class or as a take-home assignment.

Answer

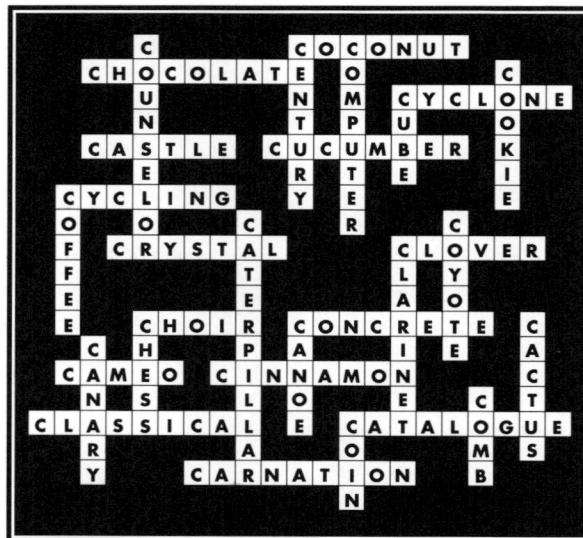

"A kind of" Crossword Puzzle

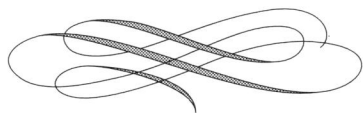

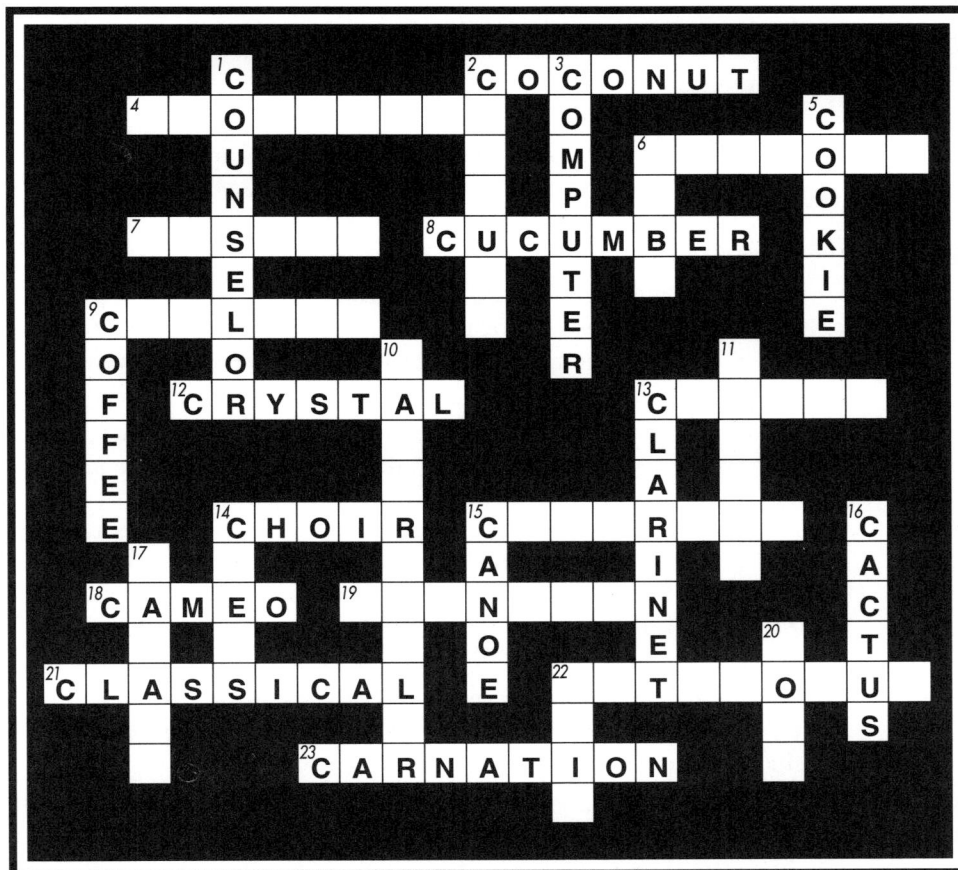

Across

2. A kind of fruit; it's hard
8. A kind of vegetable; it's long
12. A kind of glass; it's clear
14. A kind of group; it's harmonious
18. A kind of jewelry; it's carved
21. A kind of music; it's beautiful
23. A kind of flower; it's red, pink or white

Down

1. A kind of job; it's important
3. A kind of machine; it's smart
5. A kind of snack; it's round
9. A kind of drink; it's black
13. A kind of musical instrument; it's black
15. A kind of boat; it's long
16. A kind of plant; it's thorny

Helpful Language

What's number ___ across / down?

Give me another hint, (please).

What's the 2nd (3rd, 4th, 5th, 6th, 7th, 8th, 9th) letter?

How do you spell _____ ?

©North Star Publishing Co. 1995
Published by Heinemann English Language Teaching. This sheet may be photocopied and used within the class.

24

It's Debatable

Aim

To give fluency practice and encourage students to take part in a structured debate on some common social topics.

Language

Statements of opinion + language of disagreement

Preparation

This discussion-based activity needs to be explained carefully. A debate is a contest of words; an objective judge (the teacher) must be convinced of the merit of a team's arguments.

Copy Worksheet 24 onto larger paper and hand one to every student. Look at the topic line. A topic needs to be clearly two-sided and to propose a change, e.g., *The minimum drinking age should be raised*. Have students suggest possible topics. Write them on the board.

A debate requires two teams of two: the Pros and the Cons. The Pros support the change and point to the problems in the status quo. The Cons prefer the status quo and produce arguments against the Pros' reasons.

Divide the class in half. Pick one of the topics on the board and ask one half, the Pro team, for two or three reasons for change. Write these on the board. Then have the other half, the Con team, argue against these reasons. For example, the Pro team might say *Too many health problems are caused by teenagers drinking, Teenagers who drink often drive, thus causing deaths*. The Con team must take each point in turn and disprove or deny it. For example, *There are no health problems caused by teenagers who drink. Teenagers are physically active and have no money for alcohol …*

On the worksheet, this process of denial is indicated by arrows. After the denial, the Con team offers new reasons NOT to change, for example *Raising the minimum drinking age will not stop teenagers drinking*. The Pro team must then disagree directly with this point and so on.

The second stage shown on the worksheet is *The Plan*, the way to implement the change. The Pro team must put forward points stating clearly how and when the change will take place, who will be affected and how to pay for it. The Con team then attacks each point of the plan, arguing that it won't or can't work. The Con speaker then offers any final comments that he/she may feel are important.

Procedure

1. Pair the students and then put two pairs together. Let them decide on the topic and who the Pros and Cons are.

2. Allow about ten minutes for teams to prepare their arguments. They should write their ideas on the worksheet.

3. Start the debate. The first Pro speaker reads the topic and gives reasons for change.

4. The first Con speaker denies the reasons and offers reasons for no change.

5. The second Pro speaker disagrees with these reasons and introduces the plan.

6. The second Con speaker attacks each point in the plan and concludes.

Variations

1. Set a time limit for each speaker, for example five minutes each.

2. Allow the teams to speak as a team, not one at a time, in order. This will help lower ability students and less fluent groups.

Further Practice

Between one class and the next, encourage students to find some support for their reasons from newspapers and/or magazines. At a later date, repeat the same debate but this time using some evidence rather than just opinions.

It's Debatable

Topic: _____

PRO 1 Reasons for change
1) _____
2) _____
3) _____
4) _____
5) _____

CON 1 Disagreement:
1) _____
2) _____
3) _____
4) _____
5) _____

Reasons against change

PRO 2 Disagreement:
1) _____
2) _____
3) _____
4) _____
5) _____

THE PLAN
How to change:
1) _____
2) _____
3) _____
4) _____
5) _____

Why the PLAN won't work:
1) _____
2) _____
3) _____
4) _____
5) _____

CON 2 Final Comments
1) _____
2) _____
3) _____
4) _____
5) _____

©North Star Publishing Co. 1995
Published by Heinemann English Language Teaching. This sheet may be photocopied and used within the class.

What's the Question?

Aim

To practice forming *Wh-* questions accurately.

Language

Who, What, Where, When, How, How many, What kind of, etc.

Preparation

Prior to class, copy Worksheets 25a and 25b and cut them into individual cards for use as a flash-card quiz. Unlike regular quizzes, however, this activity has students formulate the correct questions. This is good practice for drilling students on the use of *Who, What, When, Where, How, How many, What kind of*, etc. questions.

Demonstrate how this works by reading one or two of the answers on the cards and helping students phrase an appropriate question. Offer other styles of questions that would also be appropriate. For example, using the answer *365 (days)*, appropriate questions might include *How many days are there in a year?* or *How long is a year?* Carefully point out that the response must be phrased as a question; if a student simply says *A year*, the response doesn't qualify since it is not a question.

Procedure

1. Divide the class into teams.

2. Explain that the first team to offer an appropriate question for a card will be awarded a point. The team with the most points after all the cards have been used is the winner.

3. Display each card in turn so that each team can see it. If the class is large, write the answer from the card on the board or, for listening practice, read it.

Variations

1. When finished, give the students blank cards and have them create their own questions on one side and with answers on the other. Have groups quiz each other.

2. Reverse the wording of the answers and the questions. For example, the card that has the answer is *The Nile* and then the question *What is the longest river in the world?* is reversed to form an answer like *It is the longest river in the world*. The question therefore becomes *What is the Nile?*

3. Offer exceedingly common answers such as *It has four legs, It's round, It's cold*, etc., and have groups of students compete against each other to call out or write down as many appropriate questions to the answer as possible.

Further Practice

To give students practice forming questions, see *Tic Tac Toe* 1 (Worksheet 10).

What's the Question?

A: Yes: "To be, or not to be – that is the question."

Q: What is a famous line from Hamlet?

A: 3.14

Q: What is the value of pi (π)?

A: The Nile.

Q: What is the longest river in the world?

A: *Oliver Twist, David Copperfield, A Tale of Two Cities.*

Q: What are three books by Charles Dickens?

A: She had to be home by midnight.

Q: What time did Cinderella have to get home?

A: It's the capital city of France.

Q: What is Paris?

A: Portuguese.

Q: What language is spoken in Portugal (or Brazil)?

A: 0°C. and 100°C.

Q: What are the freezing and boiling points of water?

A: Mt. Everest.

Q: What is the highest mountain in the world?

A: 26 (letters).

Q: How many letters are there in the English alphabet?

What's the Question?

A: 365 (days) – or– 366 (days).
Q: How many days are there in a year? –Or– (...in a leap year?)

A: Yes. Marigold, pansy, geranium.
Q: Can you name three flowers?

A: It has six strings.
Q: How many strings does a guitar have?

A: H_2O.
Q: What is water? – or – What is the chemical symbol for water?

A: Ruble, peso and rupee.
Q: What are the names of three kinds of money?

A: Yes. *Yesterday, Yellow Submarine, Let it Be.*
Q: Can you name three songs by the Beatles?

A: It has 88 keys.
Q: How many keys are there on a piano?

A: Yes. Poodle, terrier, collie.
Q: Can you name three kinds of dogs?

A: It has eight legs.
Q: How many legs does an octopus have?

©North Star Publishing Co. 1995
Published by Heinemann English Language Teaching. This sheet may be photocopied and used within the class.

Caption it!

A fat man taking a bubble bath.	Three children playing computer games.
A honeymoon couple taking pictures on the beach.	Three old men playing golf in the rain.
King Kong wearing polka-dot pajamas in New York.	A student coming late to English class.
An old woman riding her bicycle on a snowy day.	An office worker reading the sports page on a train.
Two mosquitoes planning to attack a sunbather.	A shy boy giving a Valentine's Day present to a girl.

©North Star Publishing Co. 1995
Published by Heinemann English Language Teaching. This sheet may be photocopied and used within the class.

26 Caption it!

Aim

To help students recognize and produce captions as distinct from complete sentences.

Language

Nouns to identify people and verbs used in the *-ing* form to describe their activities

Preparation

Copy Worksheets 26a and 26b and cut into cards prior to class. Introduce this exercise by explaining that titles and captions are often not complete sentences. The titles on the worksheets are good examples. *A fat man taking a bubble bath* is not a complete sentence because the verb is removed. It may be helpful to discuss and practice the use or the construction of complete sentences. To demonstrate this, show students some newspaper headlines or picture captions where the sentence is not complete.

Procedure

1. When ready, give students one card each and a blank sheet of paper.

2. On the blank sheet, have them draw the situation as described on the card. Explain that no words are to be written in their illustrations. Allow two or three minutes.

3. Collect the cards and pictures. Select one of the pictures (identify the artist) and show it to the class.

4. Have the students try to determine the situation and, ultimately the caption, by asking the artist questions. For example, if the situation is *Three children playing computer games*, students might ask questions such as: *Is that a TV? Is it a computer? Are the people old? Are they children?* The questioning continues until someone can offer a caption similar to that written on the card.

Variations

1. Establish a rule that the artist can only reply with *Yes* or *No*.

2. Try first person questions and answers like *Are you wearing glasses? Is this you? Is this your girlfriend next to you?*

3. Once pictures are drawn, pair students and have them question each other, discover the title and write it down. When finished, have students rotate to a new partner. Note: One blank card is provided on Worksheet 26b.

4. Have students create their own description cards – collect them and randomly hand them out.

5. Don't identify the artist and have students guess.

Further Practice

Before class, prepare a handful of pictures cut out of newspapers or magazines. In class, hand slips of paper to groups of students then hand each group one of the pictures. Have them write an appropriate caption for their picture. Have groups keep their captions but rotate the picture to another group. Repeat the process three or four times. When finished, hold up one of the pictures and see how the captions compare. This is a good discussion topic because different groups will see different things in the picture.

Caption it!

An old man feeding pigeons in the park.	An elementary school student day-dreaming about the summer vacation.
Dracula looking for a drink in a bar.	A young man buying a head of lettuce at the supermarket.
Santa stuck in a chimney.	Three young boys camping in the woods.
Four tired tourists looking at Big Ben.	A young couple buying engagement rings in a department store.
A couch potato eating junk food.	

©North Star Publishing Co. 1995
Published by Heinemann English Language Teaching. This sheet may be photocopied and used within the class.

27

Intern Psychologist

Aim

To practice describing things.

Language

Adjectives to describe size, condition, feelings, etc.

Preparation

This lesson encourages students to describe in detail what they see as they are led through a mental journey. In so doing, elements of their inner personality may be revealed in a non-threatening and very enjoyable way.

Procedure

1. Hand out copies of both worksheets to every student. Explain that this is a mental journey. As each situation is approached, the students will close their eyes and take a detailed mental snapshot of it before opening their eyes. Then they will write the details (using adjectives) in the appropriate places.

2. Begin by saying, *You are walking down a long, long road.* At this point, pause long enough for students to picture the road in their imagination. Have them fill in the information on the sheet according to the first box.

3. When finished, have the students close their eyes again and continue with the journey: *You walk for a long time and suddenly you see a key on the road.* Again, pause and have the students take a mental picture of the key and write a detailed description of the key. Continue leading the students from situation to situation. Use the following as a guide:

You continue walking down the road for a long time. Suddenly the road stops. You walk past the end of the road and suddenly you see an animal. You walk past the animal and keep on walking. Then you see some water. You continue walking. As you walk, you see a structure/building of some sort. You continue walking and you go up a small hill. Standing on the top, you see a person.

4. Approach the first situation (the road) by asking students to describe what they saw. Reading from their notes, encourage students to form complete sentences. Encourage other students to ask further questions about the details. When all students have finished, offer an interpretation.

Key to the meanings

(Note: these are NOT to be believed with 100 percent accuracy)

road	how you think of your life right now	water	your experiences and/or dreams of love/romance
key	how you think of your intelligence	structure	how you value material things and the importance you place on them
barrier	how you think of death (the end of the road)	person	a) someone deeply respected; b) someone deeply loved; c) someone the student would like to become
animal	how you deal with problems in life		

Variations

1. Before telling the students the meaning of each situation, see if they can guess the psychoanalytical symbolism themselves.

2. Try having the students interpret their own or each other's situations after a few models have been given by the teacher.

Further Practice

Have students take their notes home and convert them into a diary, from the first situation to the last. Students could also be asked to write an interpretation of their own journey. (In writing the interpretation, students should use synonyms which is a good way to improve their vocabulary.

Intern Psychologist

Road

Condition:

Made of:

Width:

Surroundings:

Time of day:

General feeling:

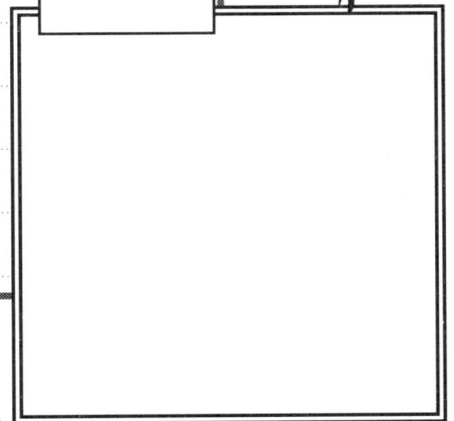

Size:

Made of:

Age:

Condition:

Action:

What:

Size:

Made of:

Beyond:

Action:

General feeling:

©North Star Publishing Co. 1995
Published by Heinemann English Language Teaching. This sheet may be photocopied and used within the class.

Intern Psychologist

Kind:

Number of:

Mood:

Animal's action:

My action:

What:

Size:

Condition:

Depth:

My action:

What:

Size:

Condition:

My mood:

My action:

Who:

Appearance:

My feeling:

My action:

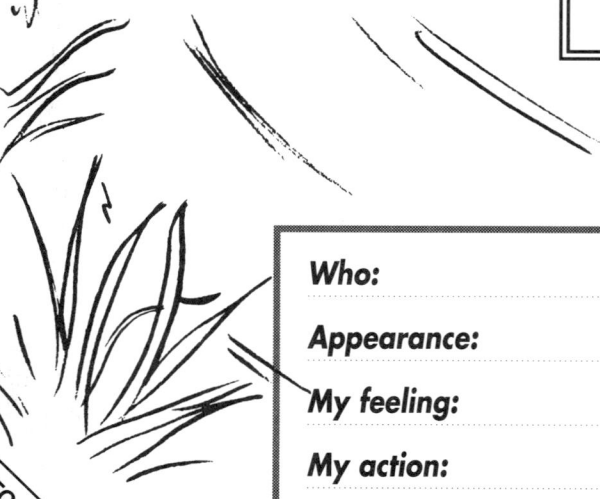

PHOTOCOPIABLE

When was the first time you ...? 28a

Follow-up questions
Who, Whose, What, Where, Why, Which, How ?

small red bicycle
from his father

Answers

six years old
was in elementary school

Example:
When was the first time you rode a bicycle?

1. rode a bicycle?
2. wrote a letter?
3. stayed in a hospital?
4. had a job?
5. kissed someone?
6. drank coffee?
7. started a diet?
8. stayed up all night?
9. talked to a foreigner?
10. lost something valuable?
11. bought something expensive?
12. had a date?
13. ... ?

©North Star Publishing Co. 1995
Published by Heinemann English Language Teaching. This sheet may be photocopied and used within the class.

When was the first time you ...?

Aim

To practice using the simple past tense with time expressions referring to earlier periods in the speaker's life.

Language

Verbs in the simple past; *When I was/did ...*, etc.

Preparation

This pairwork exercise is a follow-up to *When was the last time you ...?* and is intended for use of the simple past tense when discussing experiences in the distant past. The questions are designed to jog students' memories about events experienced earlier in life and to promote conversation about the experiences. It is thus most appropriate for higher level adult students. Example questions and answers can be put on the board.

Appropriate answers include *When I was a child, When I was a high school student, When I visited Italy*, etc. Also, *I don't/can't remember, I forget, I have never ...* .

By its nature this pairwork is more demanding than its companion, *When Was the Last Time You ...?*, and therefore follow-up and alternative questions will in many cases be necessary. Conversational gambits can be demonstrated. For example, *When was the first time you wrote a letter? What was it about? Was it a love letter? For whom? Where is that person now? Do you like to write letters? How often do you write a letter?* etc.

Procedure

1. Pair the students and hand out Worksheets 28a and 28b, one to each student respectively.

2. Have them ask each other the *When was the first time you ...?* questions and write their partner's response in the appropriate space.

3. Then, students should ask at least one follow-up question and write this response in the appropriate space.

4. Finally, have students think of one additional question for line 13.

Note Through the use of follow-up questions, some students may become quite involved in a conversation about that event. This, of course, should be encouraged – even if students don't finish the entire list.

Variations

1. When finished, split the pairs apart and form new pairs. Have students ask third-person questions about their new partner's former partner.

2. Use as a *Crossfire* exercise with paired partners sitting in groups of four as if at a card table. Partners sit diagonal to each other. Questions are asked simultaneously with the two teams competing to be heard over their competitors and racing to the finish.

Further Practice

See *When was the last time you ...?* (Worksheet 22)

Using the pattern *When was the first time you ...?* have students refer to the prompts for *Can you ...?* (Worksheets 18a and 18b).

Have students write a short biographical account of any one of the experiences as related by their partners. These could be read to the class.

When was the first time you ...?

Answers

sixteen years old
was a high school student

Follow-up questions

Who, Whose, What, Where, Why, Which, How ?

with two friends   was cold and wet
          food was terrible

Example:
When was the first time you went camping?

1. went camping?

2. read a novel?

3. drove a car?

4. played a musical instrument?

5. went to a wedding?

6. cooked dinner by yourself?

7. bought a piece of furniture?

8. drank alcohol?

9. went to a disco?

10. fell in love?

11. used a credit card?

12. took an overnight trip alone?

13. ... _____ ?

©North Star Publishing Co. 1995
Published by Heinemann English Language Teaching. This sheet may be photocopied and used within the class.

29 Education

Aim

To introduce students to related word forms.

Language

Verbs with related noun forms ending in *-ation, -tion,* or *-ion*

Preparation

For intermediate and advanced students, this lesson is useful in demonstrating how they can make their English more sophisticated by using noun forms of verbs. Write the word *educate* on the board. Explain that the noun form of *educate* is *education*. Point out that many verbs can be changed into nouns by simply adding *-ation, -tion,* or *-ion* as a suffix. Write a few of the verb forms on the board and have students offer some noun counterparts. Then have students compose two sentences, one with the verb form and the other with the noun form, for example *How do you abbreviate the word Avenue?* Students write answers such as *The abbreviation of the word* Avenue *is* Ave. Write these on the board as well.

Procedure

1. Copy and hand out Worksheet 29 to all of the students. Go through the verbs beginning with *A* first with the whole class supplying the noun forms of *abbreviate, associate,* and *act.*

2. Ask students to suggest another *A* verb that can be made into a noun with *-ation, -tion,* or *-ion,* for example *accumulation, application, automation.*

3. Pair students and have them arrive at the noun form for the rest of the verbs.

4. On the right is a blank space for students to think up their own verbs and accompanying noun forms. The list is roughly alphabetical so new words should begin with the same letter of the alphabet as the other three in the list.

Variations

1. Before handing out the worksheet, read the list, one word at a time, and have the students convert the verbs to nouns.

2. Make this a competitive pairwork activity by having each pair race to find all of the noun forms or race to fill in all of the blanks in the right-hand column.

Answers

Noun Forms

abbreviation	association	action	congratulation	creation
collection	direction	domination	determination	examination
exhibition	elimination	foundation	formulation	frustration
generation	graduation	generalization	humanization	harmonization
hospitalization	imagination	isolation	internationalization	limitation
location	liberalization	modernization	maximization	motivation
nationalization	nomination	narration	operation	observation
organization	production	protection	pronunciation	restoration
realization	reduction	standardization	separation	situation
translation	transportation	termination		

Further Practice

1. As a review, read off five or so verbs each lesson and have students convert them to their noun forms.

2. Have pairs of students practice using an assigned number of the new noun forms in sentences or even as a newspaper article.

Education

BACK to School

Change these verbs into nouns:

Another word

abbreviate	associate	act	. . . .
congratulate	create	collect	. . . .
direct	dominate	determine	. . . .
examine	exhibit	eliminate	. . . .
found	formulate	frustrate	. . . .
generate	graduate	generalize	. . . .
humanize	harmonize	hospitalize	. . . .
imagine	isolate	internationalize	. . . .
limit	locate	liberalize	. . . .
modernize	maximize	motivate	. . . .
nationalize	nominate	narrate	. . . .
operate	observe	organize	. . . .
produce	protect	pronounce	. . . .
restore	realize	reduce	. . . .
standardize	separate	situate	. . . .
translate	transport	terminate	. . . .

Irregular Verb Word Search 2

Aim

To reinforce knowledge of present and past tense forms of irregular verbs.

Language

40 irregular verbs

Preparation

Students approaching this exercise should be well grounded in the basic 80 or 90 English irregular verbs and know their present and past tense forms. This word search puzzle is useful as a reinforcement of their knowledge. Before handing out the Worksheet 30, read down the list of verbs in the present tense and have students say their past tense form. (This could be done in teams to make this part competitive, giving a point to the team which answers first.)

Also, teach the following three words: *horizontal(ly)*, *vertical(ly)* and *diagonal(ly)*.

Procedure

1. Pair the students and have them fold their papers along the dotted line separating part A from part B.

2. One student looks at the word search puzzle at the top, the other looks at the verbs at the bottom. Student B begins by asking: *What's the past tense of lend?* Student A responds with: *(The past tense of lend is) lent*.

3. Then Student A looks for the word *went* which is printed somewhere in the puzzle. If Student A has trouble finding the word, he/she can ask for a hint: *Where is it?* Student B looks at the hint as printed on his/her paper: G15–v and responds with: *It begins on G15 and goes vertically*.

Variations

1. As a whole class (or competitive group) activity, appoint one student to be the MC and hand one copy to each of the other students. Have everyone fold the papers horizontally and all but the MC look at Part A. The MC looks only at Part B. The MC reads the present tense verbs and students search for their past tense forms. When each is found, the student reveals its location by saying, for example: *It begins on K3 and goes horizontally*. The MC confirms the answer.

2. This can be done as a take-home assignment but before making copies, blank out the hints from part B (otherwise it's too easy).

Answers

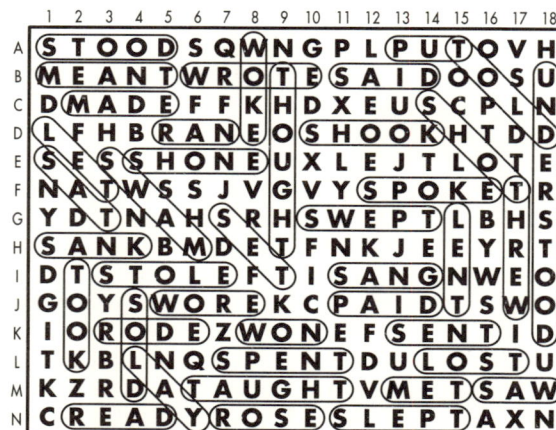

Further Practice

See *Irregular Verb Word Search 1* (Worksheet 4).

Irregular Verb Word Search 2

30

A

	1	2	3	4	5	6	7	8	9	10	11	12	13	14	15	16	17	18
A	S	T	O	O	D	S	Q	W	N	G	P	L	P	U	T	O	V	H
B	M	E	A	N	T	W	R	O	T	E	S	A	I	D	O	O	S	U
C	D	M	A	D	E	F	F	K	H	D	X	E	U	S	C	P	L	N
D	L	F	H	B	R	A	N	E	O	S	H	O	O	K	H	T	D	D
E	S	E	S	S	H	O	N	E	U	X	L	E	J	T	L	O	T	E
F	N	A	T	W	S	S	J	V	G	V	Y	S	P	O	K	E	T	R
G	Y	D	T	N	A	H	S	R	H	S	W	E	P	T	L	B	H	S
H	S	A	N	K	B	M	D	E	T	F	N	K	J	E	E	Y	R	T
I	D	T	S	T	O	L	E	F	T	I	S	A	N	G	N	W	E	O
J	G	O	Y	S	W	O	R	E	K	C	P	A	I	D	T	S	W	O
K	I	O	R	O	D	E	Z	W	O	N	E	F	S	E	N	T	I	D
L	T	K	B	L	N	Q	S	P	E	N	T	D	U	L	O	S	T	U
M	K	Z	R	D	A	T	A	U	G	H	T	V	M	E	T	S	A	W
N	C	R	E	A	D	Y	R	O	S	E	S	L	E	P	T	A	X	N

horizontal ←——→   vertical ↕   diagonal ↖↘

B

Hints & Answers

	Present Tense	Past Tense		Present Tense	Past Tense		Present Tense	Past Tense
G15–v	lend	*lent*	M16–h	see		A1–h	stand	
D1–d	let	*let*	J4–v	sell		G10–h	sweep	
L4–d	lie		K13–h	send		E3–d	swim	
L14–h	lose		G7–d	set		I2–v	take	
C2–h	make		I11–h	sing		M6–h	teach	
B1–h	mean		H1–h	sink		A15–d	tell	
M13–h	meet		E1–d	sit		B9–v	think	
J11–h	pay		D10–h	shake		F17–v	throw	
A13–h	put		E4–h	shine		B18–v	understand	
N2–h	read		C14–d	shoot		A8–v	wake	
K3–h	ride		N11–h	sleep		J5–h	wear	
N7–h	rise		F12–h	speak		K8–h	win	
D5–h	run		I3–h	steal		B6–h	write	
B11–h	say		L7–h	spend				

h=horizontal ←——→   v=vertical ↕   d=diagonal ↖↘

©North Star Publishing Co. 1995
Published by Heinemann English Language Teaching. This sheet may be photocopied and used within the class.

31 Postcards

Aim

To write postcards describing typical vacation experiences.

Language

Vocabulary of vacations and hotels
Adjectives that express positive and negative opinions

Preparation

Writing sample postcards in English is good practice for the time when students actually do take a trip somewhere and want to write to classmates or the teacher. There are two postcards in this lesson; in the top one students complain about things concerning their vacation and in the bottom one, students describe favorable things.

Begin with a discussion about vacations. Ask students where they've gone, what was bad, what was good. On the board, write the words *food, hotel, people* and *transportation*. Ask students to provide one more category such as *weather, sightseeing* or *shopping*; add this word to those on the board. Have students offer adjectives for each describing something bad and something good. For example, the food could be *expensive, salty and cold* or *cheap, delicious and hot*. The hotel could be *dirty, small and noisy* or *clean, large and quiet*, etc.

Procedure

1. Copy worksheet 30 onto large paper and hand one copy to each student.

2. Pair students and have them dictate their addresses to each other; these are written on the appropriate lines on the right side of both postcards.

3. Next, draw students' attention to the information boxes in the middle of the worksheet. In the left box, students should write one or two negative adjectives, in the right one, opposite, positive ones.

4. When finished, have students exchange papers. Explain that students cannot use the category words *food, hotel, people* or *transportation* in the postcard. They need to write words that fall in the category (*food: spaghetti, croissants,* etc., *hotel: lobby, room, swimming pool,* etc.).

5. Have them write the upper postcard using the information in the left box:

> *Dear _____ ,*
>
> *I arrived here yesterday and I'm tired. The spaghetti was expensive, the lobby was dirty, the receptionist was unfriendly, the taxi was too slow and the temperature was cold.*

6. Encourage students to write something else in closing such as *I'm feeling a little homesick, I wish I were somewhere else, I wish you were here*. Then have students sign their name at the bottom.

7. Repeat the process for Postcard 2. All the adjectives, however, are positive.

Variations

1. When all students have finished, have partners exchange papers, split apart and pair up with someone new. Using the postcards, have them discuss in the third person their first partner's vacations. For example, *Where did he/she go? What did he/she say about the food/the hotel/the people/the transportation?*

2. Use the completed postcards as a pairwork dictation exercise by giving all students a second, blank copy of the lesson and having partners dictate the contents of the postcards to each other.

Further Practice

1. See *Opposites* 1 (Worksheet 7) and *Opposites* 2 (Worksheet 19).

2. Give students real postcards and have them pretend to be on vacation somewhere. Have students actually send the postcards through the mail.

POST*CARD* 1

Dear   ,   /   /

I arrived here yesterday and
I'm tired. The

Sincerely,

Name

Address

50c

POST*CARD* 1 (Information)

Food: _____
Hotel: _____
People: _____
Transportation: _____
Other: _____

POST*CARD* 2 (Information)

Food: _____
Hotel: _____
People: _____
Transportation: _____
Other: _____

POST*CARD* 2

Dear   ,   /   /

I'm feeling much better today

Sincerely,

Name

Address

PHOTOCOPIABLE

32

Dial-a-Word

Aim

To practice spelling simple messages, saying lists of single digits as in telephone numbers and decoding short messages.

Language

Letters and numbers

Preparation

Copy and hand out Worksheet 32 to each student so that they can see the lettering system on an American telephone. Explain that the alphabet as printed is often an effective method to remember certain telephone numbers. Advertisers, for example, often work out a word or words which are easy to remember. A telephone number is usually more difficult to remember than a word. For example, a TV commercial for a carpet company could advertise by saying *Please dial 227-7387*. However, *Please dial C-A-R-P-E-T-S* is so much easier to remember. Another business might say *Please dial P-E-T • S-H-O-P (738-7467)*.

On the board, write a few coded messages such as *2255-666 (C-A-L-L • M-O-M)*, *74663-63 (P-H-O-N-E • M-E)*, and/or *4-5683-968 (I • L-O-V-E • Y-O-U)*. Help the students work through these codes by demonstrating that in English certain consonants seldom or never go together at the beginning of words. For example, *2255 (CALL)*; the initial 22 could be *AA*, *BB* or *CC* but not likely (except for *aardvark*). *BC*, *CB* are not possible leaving only *AB*, *AC*, *BA* or *CA*.

Procedure

1. Put the students into groups of four and have each one write one short message (numbers only) on the line titled *Messages*. The message could be one, two or three words (or more), but each word should not have too many letters because that increases the difficulty of decoding it.

2. When finished, each student reads his/her coded message and the others write it on one of the lines provided on the left.

3. Then have students work at decoding the messages.

Variations

1. See if students can write a coded message using their own telephone numbers.

2. Have pairs of students compose sentence messages to give to other pairs.

3. Prior to class, prepare five or six simple coded messages. In class, divide the students into teams, write the codes, one at a time on the board and have them compete against each other to be the first to decode the message.

Further Practice

1. Write a sentence or paragraph on the board but code all of the nouns, verbs or adjectives, etc.

2. Have groups of students plan a 20–30 second TV commercial or an advertisement in the Yellow Pages where they advertise their products using a word or words for the phone number.

DIAL-a-WORD ㉜

(3425-2-9673)

1
2 ABC
3 DEF
4 GHI
5 JKL
6 MNO
7 PRS
8 TUV
9 WXY
*
0 OPERATOR
#
CODES
MESSAGES
ANSWERS
1.
2.
3.
4.
1.
2.
3.
4.

Class Models

Aim

To get students co-operating with each other in creating group scenes.

Language

Parts of the body

Verbs of movement

Giving instructions

Labels identifying roles, situations, etc.

Preparation

In this lesson, students direct other students to model certain poses as if they were choreographing a scene for a still photograph. To add additional impact to the lesson, bring a camera to class.

Students should have gone through *Synchronized English* (Worksheets 35a and 35b) before doing this lesson, which serves not only as a review but also as an extension.

Procedure

1. Hand out Worksheet 33 and pair the students. Beginning with the first box, have students draw figures according to the description. In the second box, have students work together to write out a description of what two people must do to be in the position as shown in the drawing. Students continue through the third and fourth box.

2. Next, review verbs which indicate movement – this will become important as students direct the positioning of their classmates.

3. Group the students into threes. In the framed box at the bottom of the worksheet, each student draws a two-person scene (that will be choreographed later in the class). The scenes should be captioned. Encourage students to create an interesting scene such as *Jack kills the giant*, *The Safari*, *The Lifeguard*, etc.

4. Each student in turn assumes the role of the camera person; the other two people in his/her group are the models. The camera person then directs the models into position according to his/her sketch. When the two are positioned correctly, the camera person takes the picture. Other students in class try to guess the caption.

Variations

1. After doing this lesson and *The Proposal* (Worksheets 14a and 14b), have students choreograph a romantic proposal using two other students in class.

2. Make larger groups so that three, four, or five models will need to be positioned.

Further Practice

1. At a later date, after the photos have been processed, group the students and have them show their photos. The members of the group then describe the positioning of the models to review and reinforce the language.

2. For a review of parts of the body, see *I Bet You Can't* (Worksheet 36).

3. To practice using vocabulary of placement and positioning, see *Synchronized English* (Worksheets 35a and 35b).

Class Models

1. The Choke Hold

Jim, sit on a chair with your left leg over your right leg. Chris, stand behind Jim with your left hand on his right shoulder and your right arm around his neck.

2. Dancing

3. The Car Accident

Sam, lie on your back with your legs apart and your right hand on your head. Put your left arm straight out at your side. Frieda, kneel on Sam's left side with your left hand under his head and your right ear on his chest.

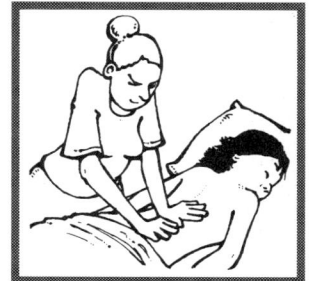

4. The Massage

Design a Photograph

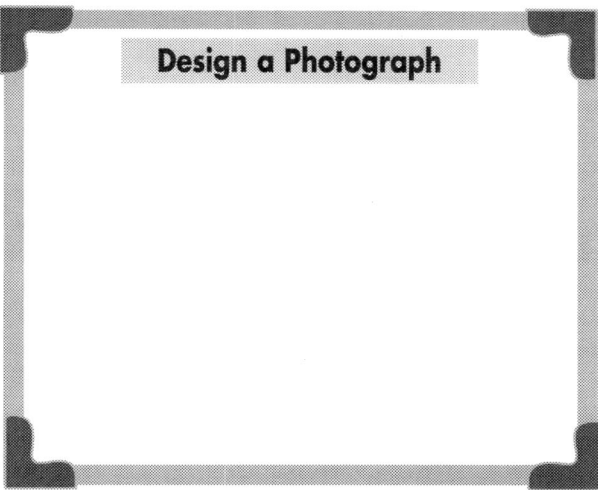

Caption

Giving Instructions

 *move farther apart*

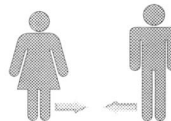 *move closer together*

move forward/move towards the camera

move back/move away from the camera

move a little to your right/left

stand behind/in front of him/her

Mini-summit

Aim

To review some standardized conversational exchanges.

Language

Greetings, introductions, ways of saying goodbye, etc.

Preparation

This lesson is a quick review of greetings, responses, introductions and good-byes. Ask students to suggest places where strangers might meet for the first time. Using one of the suggestions, roleplay a greeting with a few of the students. Greet them with a simple *Hi, Hello,* or *Good afternoon.* Students should respond in kind. Then extend the greeting with a question such as *How are you?* or *How's it going?* Students should respond with *Great! Fine, Pretty good,* etc. Go through introductions and responses. then continue with closings and finally saying goodbye.

Point out that when someone begins to say goodbye, for example, *Well, I've got to be going now,* it's not uncommon for someone to ask why. At this point, the speaker needs to come up with a reason for leaving. Have students offer a few reasons and write these on the board. Copy Worksheet 34.

Procedure

1. Pair students and hand out the worksheet. Together, students read through the contents of each of the clouds and then assign a sequential number to each cloud according to a natural process of greeting, introduction, closing a conversation and saying good-bye. (The fourth cloud is numbered on the worksheet.) Point out that within each cloud, there are a number of interchangeable phrases.

2. When pairs have finished assigning numbers 1–3 and 5–7, direct their attention to the upper right cloud as printed. These are the elements of the conversation, the *Where, Who,* and *Why.* Students write in an interesting place where strangers might meet for the first time, for example, on the top floor of a burning building or on a ski-lift. Then have them fill in the names of two people or characters and finally write a reason for leaving. When finished, tell the students to tear their papers along the vertical line (see *cut here*).

3. Beginning with the first block *Place,* on the torn-off page, students write the same thing they wrote next to *Place* in the cloud. Then have them fold the *Place* block back and rotate their papers one to the right, and write one (only one) of the elements found in Cloud 1, for example *Hi! Hello,* etc. Then, students fold the A-block back and rotate the papers again. Students continue by writing one of the elements from Cloud 1 in the B-block. The process continues, using a phrase from the cloud specified, until all of the blocks have been filled in.

Next, have students unfold the entire sheet. Beginning with one student (Student A) have him/her read the place and then alternately read through the conversation from his/her sheet with another student (Student B).

Variations

1. In the original pairs, have students alternately read parts A + B from their own sheets.

2. Encourage pairs of students to memorize their papers and act out the scene.

3. Have students turn over the Mini-summit worksheet and hand out blank copies of the tear-off conversation section. Encourage students to write a conversation with these five parts: 1) Greeting + Response, 2) Greeting Question + Response, 3) Self Introduction + Response, 4) Closing + Response (Why?) and 5) Saying Goodbye.

Mini-summit

4

I'm _____

My name is _____

Place: _____
Person A: _____
Person B: _____
Reasons for leaving: *Because* _____

☐

So long. | Take care.

Goodbye. | See you.

Have fun! | Good luck.

Catch you later.

Excellent.

How's it going?

OK. | Good.

☐ How are you doing?

Great. | Wonderful.

How are you?

Fine. | So so.

How do you do?

Not bad.

☐ Nice meeting you.

Spectacular. | Pretty good.

I'm afraid I must be going now.

☐

Sorry, but I've got to run.

Hello. | Hi!

Well, I've got to go now.

Hi there. | Good afternoon.

Place: ☐

A: Cloud 1

B: Cloud 1

A: Cloud 2

B: How about you? Cloud 3

A: Cloud 3

B: By the way, Cloud 4

A: Cloud 5

A: Cloud 4

B: Cloud 5

A: Cloud 6

B: Why? Reason

A: Because, Cloud 7

B: OK, Cloud 7

A:

PHOTOCOPIABLE

Synchronized English

Aim

To demonstrate comprehension of other students' instructions by movement or by pictures.

Language

Parts of the body

Simple instructions

Preparation

This activity introduces 44 physical positions and the language used to describe them. Begin by performing some of the sample positions from Worksheet 35a and have the students describe them.

Procedure

1. Hand out a copy of Worksheet 35a to every student. Invite two or three students to stand at the front of the room (without their worksheets). The other students read off the positions, one at a time, and the students at the front of the room, in synchronization, follow the instructions.

2. Then pair the students and hand out copies of Worksheet 35b. Together, students practice the language by drawing the positions described in boxes numbered 1, 3 and 5. Students write a description for boxes numbered 2, 4 and 6.

3. When students have become familiar with the language, have pairs design Position A and Position B, one drawing the position and the other writing it in words. Pairs of students then describe their Positions 1 and 2 while their classmates follow the instructions in synchronization.

Variations

1. Have students describe the positions either with their backs turned to the rest of the class or from somewhere in the room where the rest of the class can't be seen. During the description, the other students in class follow the instructions in synchronization.When finished, have the pairs confirm their accuracy by looking at their classmates.

2. Students think of a common pose such as the beginning of a golf swing, fishing, reading a newspaper, and describe this position to the others in the class who act out the instructions. The first student to identify the pose is awarded a point.

3. Before making multiple copies, white out half of the words (and/or pictures) on one copy of Worksheet 35a and the other half on another copy. Then pair the students, hand out two different sheets and have them exchange the missing information and write it down.

Further practice

1. For a review of body parts, see *I Bet you Can't*, Worksheet 36.

2. For reinforcement and extension of this lesson, see *Class Models*, Worksheet 33.

Synchronized English

look right	look left	look up	look down	look straight ahead
tilt your head to the right	tilt your head to the left	cross your arms	put your arms straight out at your sides	put your arms down at your sides
put your arms straight up over your head	put your arms straight out (in front of you)	put your arms straight out with your elbows bent up	put your hands in your pockets	put your hands on top of your head
put your hands on your hips	put your hands on your shoulders	put your hands behind your head	put your hands over your face	put your hands behind your back
stand with your legs together	stand with your legs apart	stand with your left leg forward and your right leg back	stand on your left leg	stand with your legs crossed
sit on a chair	sit on a chair with your right leg over your left leg	sit on the floor with your legs crossed	sit on the floor with your knees bent	sit on the floor with your legs straight
sit on a chair with your right ankle on your left knee	stoop	kneel	get down on your hands and knees	bend over at your waist
stand on your hands	stand on your head	lean on the table with your left hand	lean against the wall with your left shoulder	
lie on your back	lie on your stomach	lie on your right side	lie on your left side	

Synchronized English

Position Combinations

①

Stoop with your legs crossed.

②

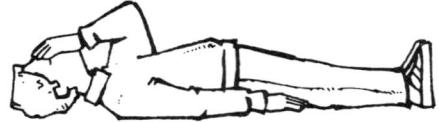

③

Stand on your left leg with your arms down at your sides, looking left.

④

⑤

Sit on a chair with your right arm behind your back and your left hand on top of your head, looking down.

⑥

Position A

Position B

©North Star Publishing Co. 1995
Published by Heinemann English Language Teaching. This sheet may be photocopied and used within the class.

I Bet You Can't!

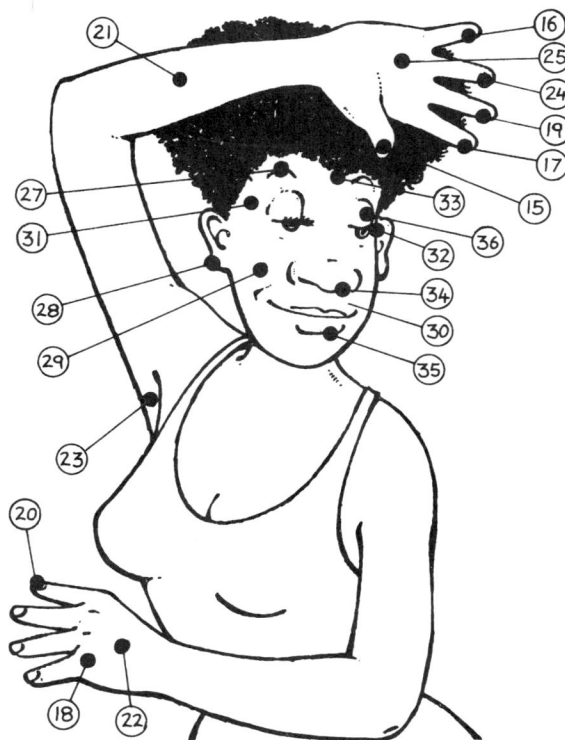

1 hand **4** wrist

2 arm **5** finger

3 elbow **6** shoulder

15 thumb

index finger

middle finger

ring finger

baby finger

finger nail

palm

back of the hand

armpit

forearm

knuckle

26

7 head **12** eye

8 hair **13** mouth

9 ear **14** nose

10 chin

11 neck

27 eyebrow

eyelid

eyelash

earlobe

forehead

upper lip

lower lip

temple

nostril

cheek

37

38

A chest **D** foot **I** stomach **J** knee

B waist **E** ankle **G** leg **H** back

C hip **F** toe

K rib

thigh

shin

calf

big toe

second toe

middle toe

fourth toe

little toe

arch

sole

heel

navel

X

Y

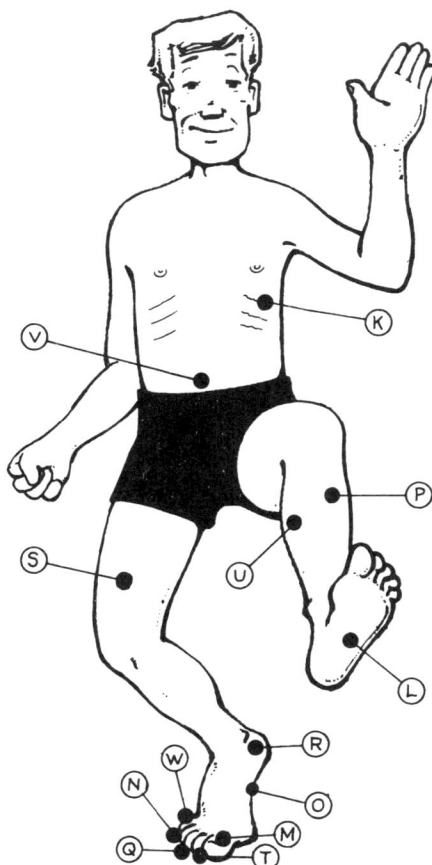

SAMPLE SENTENCES

A: I bet you can't put your nose on your right foot.

B: You want me to put my nose on my right foot?

A: Yes, that's right./No, I want you to put …

B: I bet I can./You're right, I can't.

SCORE CARD

Code	Put your …	Points
(R) (L) 28 - R	… (right) earlobe on your (left) heel.	
( ) ( )		
( ) ( )		
( ) ( )		
( ) ( )		
( ) ( )		
	Total Points	

©North Star Publishing Co. 1995
Published by **Heinemann English Language Teaching**. This sheet may be photocopied and used within the class.

I Bet You Can't!

Aim

To review the names of parts of the body in a fun and challenging way.

Language

Terms for external parts of the body

Preparation

This lesson reinforces the language involved in getting someone to do something. It is an active review of parts of the body and usually becomes competitive and exciting. With lower-level students, the teacher begins by touching or pointing to various parts of his/her body. Students say what these parts are. Higher-level students can skip this part. Next, demonstrate a sentence which combines two of the parts of the body, for example, *Put your hand on your elbow*. Introduce more specific information such as *Put your left hand on your right elbow*. Encourage students to give you a number of these commands using *Put*... Write these on the board.

Procedure

1. Copy Worksheet 36 and hand out to all students. Students write down words which are on the board but not on their worksheet in the blank spaces provided. These should be assigned a number or letter.

2. Then, beginning with the hand and face, have students match the numbers 15–36 to the words. Continue with the letters assigned to the body parts, K–W. Then challenge a few students with *I bet you can't put your eyebrow on your right heel*. Students respond with either, *I bet I can* or *You're right, I can't*. Then convert the parts of the body into their corresponding numbers and letters, for example *I bet you can't put your 23 on your M*. Students decode the sentence and respond appropriately.

3. Pair the students. Tell them the object is to get the most points by being able to do something that their partner thought they couldn't do. If a student can do what he/she is told, one point is given. If the task is impossible (*Put your right elbow on your left ear*), no point is given. Draw students' attention to the score card. Students should write five coded messages according to things they think their partner can't do. When the lists have been finished, have Student A begin by saying, *I bet you can't put your (number) on your (letter)*. Student B decodes the sentence and says, *You want me to put my right eyebrow on my left ankle?* Student A confirms the sentence by saying *Yes* or *No*. Student B then replies, *I bet I can* or *You're right, I can't*. If Student B says *You're right, I can't*, one point is marked on the score card. After all five challenges have been done, the student with the most points is the winner.

Variations

1. Introduce verbs other than *put* such as *touch, place, lay, pat, tap*.

2. Put students into groups of three. Have two students work together to challenge the other student to do something. (*We bet you can't* ....)

3. Reverse the challenge by having students think of something they think they can do and their partner earns points by correctly guessing the possibility. For example, Student A says, *I bet I can put my left ear on my right knee*. Student B says either, *I bet you can't*, or *I bet you can, too*. If Student B guesses correctly, he/she gets a point.

Further Practice

1. For practice and expansion of this activity, see *Class Models* (Worksheet 32).

2. Have students put their papers away and play *Simon Says* to review parts of the body.

Contributors

Heinemann Questionnaire

At Heinemann ELT we are committed to continuing research into materials development. We would be very interested to hear your feedback about this resource book. Please photocopy this form and send it to your local Heinemann office or to the address at the bottom of the form. Thank you for your help.

Name: ....

Name of school: ....

Address of school: ....

Average age of students: ....

Size of class: ....

Frequency and length of lesson: ......

Course materials currently used with class:

....

....

Supplementary materials currently used with class:

....

....

Please tell us if you have enjoyed using this photocopiable teacher's resource book. If not, please tell us why not; if you have, please tell us why.

....

....

....

What features do you like most about this resource book? What do you like least?

....

....

....

Do you have any suggestions for improvements?

....

....

....

What other kinds of materials would you like to see in a photocopiable format?

....

....

....

Please check the boxes below if you would like information about new materials or would like to help us in materials development.

I would like to receive information about new materials for ...

☐ children ☐ adults
☐ exams ☐ readers
☐ secondary school students
☐ university students
☐ business English
☐ supplementary materials

Would you be willing to help us develop new materials to suit your needs? Yes, I would like to ...

☐ pilot materials in my classroom.
☐ answer questionnaires.
☐ discuss my needs with a Heinemann Representative.

Please return this form to:

Editor, Heinemann Teacher Resources, Heinemann ELT, Halley Court, Jordan Hill, Oxford OX2 8EJ, UK

If you would prefer to fax the form, please send to + 44 1865 314193.

RM1 © Heinemann Publishers (Oxford) Ltd. 1995